D0472309

Come to the Boucherie ... a Focus for Family Life

"Laissez les bon temps rouler": (let the good times roll) is probably the most commonly used expression in Acadian country. It applies to almost every phase of Cajun life and goes hand in hand with hard work. A good example is "The Boucherie" (the butchering), which becomes a small celebration with the families of brothers or cousins or neighbors getting together to butcher several hogs at one time. Some of the products are cooked and eaten while the work of cutting up the meat goes on. Various kinds of Sausages are made; lard is rendered out of the cut up skin, leaving delicious "Cracklings" to be eaten as is, or used in cornbread; and Bacon, Hams and Tasso (Cajun jerky which is hotly seasoned for use in cooking with vegetables) are all produced. Everything but the squeal is used, for Fromage de Tète (Head Cheese) is made from the meat of the head and the gelatin of the feet and knuckles. All of the products shown were provided by Oak Grove Smoke House in Prairieville, Louisiana. In addition to smoking Turkeys and Chickens, they also produce seasoned mixes for making Gumbo, Jambalaya, Dirty Rice, Beignets (French Doughnuts), and many other Cajun specialties, including Crab Boil (a mixture of herbs and spices for boiling seafood).

TURNIP GREENS COOKED WITH TASSO

Use 3 or 4 bundles of turnips. Cut off turnip bottoms, peel, and dice. Pick tender parts of turnip leaves away from stems and tough ribs. Wash thoroughly more than once. Put 2 tablespoons shortening in large heavy pot and heat well. Add washed greens, and a little extra water. Cut 1/2 pound of tasso into biteable strips and fry it lightly with chopped onions in separate pan, or substitute ham, salt meat, or pickled pork cut into chunks. In South Louisiana, almost all vegetables are cooked with some form of meat.

Halfway through cooking the greens, add the diced turnips and the meat and cook until everything is tender.

To any Louisianian, the green tops are more important than the turnip bottoms, and the pot liquor is the most important of all. It is best absorbed in huge chunks of cornbread. When the meal is finished, the empty bowls should be spotless. Mustard greens, chard, kale, or any other greens may be cooked in the same manner. Some cooks like to add a light roux to the pot liquor.

(Author's Recipe)

(Check the index for any recipes that are not on the same page with the picture that shows that particular dish.)

HOW TO COOK RICE
THE CAJUN WAY

Bring at least 3 quarts of well salted water to a rapid boil. Add one tablespoon of oil and one of vinegar to water. Slowly add one cup of long grain rice (which will increase by half in bulk) which has been picked over but not washed. Reduce heat and simmer for exactly 18 minutes. The oil will keep the water from boiling over and the vinegar will let each grain "fall to itself" when served. Drain through a colander and rinse off excess starch with cold water. Return to colander and steam over a little hot water in the pot for a few minutes until well warmed again.

LINK SAUSAGE

Prick the skin of long links of sausage in quite a few places. Simmer in a little hot water until the water is gone and the sausages are well browned. They can be cut in lengths or chunks and added to the beans or served separately on the side of the plate.

RED BEANS AND RICE

1/2 pound **smoked** sausage (or more if you wish)	1 or 2 **smoked** ham hocks or a ham bone (pieces about 3" or 4")
1 pound dried kidney beans	1/2 to 1/3 lb. tasso (optional)
1 onion (equal to a cup)	2 bay leaves
2 scallions (green part)	Pinch of thyme
2 stalks celery and leaves	Salt and black pepper to taste
1/2 small Bell pepper	2 tablespoons parsley

(Chop all above vegetables)

Wash and drain beans. Add all other ingredients and bring to a boil. Turn to simmer and cook 2 to 3 hours, stirring occasionally (covered). Meanwhile, sauté sliced sausage until most of the grease is rendered. Add to beans about 20 minutes before serving. It is really best to use a whole pound of sausage.

Serve in profuse quantities ladled over fluffy long grain rice. Don't forget to lay sliced raw onions and butter on top of each plate. Be sure to use fresh beans, which should get very creamy, but most will remain whole. (Old beans will never get tender.)

Recipe from Cookin' Cajun
Cooking School in New Orleans

There's No Place Like Home ... in a Cajun Cabin

This is as typical a small Cajun cabin as one can find. They were very simple and almost always had an exterior staircase or ladder to the attic, where the older boys of the family slept. Often there was a pot shelf outside one of the side windows, so that "Maman" could set the dish pan there and keep an eye on the yard or gossip with the neighbors. Sometimes a thin curtain hung at the door, to let the breezes in and keep the insects out. Screening was not known in the early years. Those having two rooms in the front had two french doors.

Red Beans and Rice with Sausage is one of the best known Louisiana dishes. It was a great Monday meal, for one could put it on the back of the stove and let it cook while one was washing the clothes. Red beans can also be cooked with ham, bacon, salt pork or pickle meat, and are especially delicious if simmered with a-ham bone. Here it is served with a "Finger Food" Vegetable Salad and a bowl of Apples, Pears and Tangerines.

Typical Acadian Cottage in South Louisiana

ARTICHOKE AND GARLIC BALLS

Drain one can of artichoke hearts well. Chop in food processor. Chop one small onion in processor. Crush two cloves of garlic. Sauté onions in one tablespoon of butter or margarine, add chopped artichokes and garlic and continue heating. Turn off heat and add seasoned bread crumbs until you have a consistency that can be shaped into balls. Add salt and pepper to taste. Form balls and roll in bread crumbs. Fry in deep fat or brown in an oven, but frying will make them crispier. These are nice hors d'oeuvres to serve with drinks.

FINGER FOOD VEGGIE SALAD

Cut raw vegetables in long wedges. Place in large bowls with a "puddle" of salad dressing in the center and let everyone pick up the wedges and dip them in the dressing. Tomatoes, cucumbers, zucchini, yellow squash, and green onion sticks may be used, or anything else your imagination conjures up.

Pique-Nique on the Bayou

Our word "picnic" comes from the French, in which "pique" refers to the quilt, and "nique" refers to making fun. "Bayou" comes from a Choctaw Indian word, and is a lazy stream. South Louisiana is known as Bayou Country. Some are tributaries to larger rivers, and some are distributaries which run from the Mississippi to the Gulf. They account for the lushness of growth here, because everything is well watered. Cajun Catfish is the center of interest at this picnic, and is surrounded by a Broccoli, Rice and Cheese Casserole; Corn Soup with Tomatoes and River Shrimp; Stuffed Yellow Squash with Ham; Artichoke and Garlic Balls with Ripe Olives; Beignets; Dates stuffed with Cream Cheese and Pecans; Buns and Strawberry Preserves. Catfish, Shrimp, Rice, Pecans, and Strawberries are all well-known products of Louisiana. Globe Artichokes are found in many Cajun gardens and if allowed to flower, they produce a cobalt blue head like a thistle flower.

CORN SOUP WITH TOMATOES AND RIVER SHRIMP

Cut kernels off 4 ears of corn and scrape cob well, catching all corn, scrapings, and milk in a pan. Heat two cans of tomatoes or stew fresh tomatoes well, breaking up into small pieces. Add 1/3 cup chopped shallots which have been sautéed, 1/2 teaspoon basil and salt and pepper. Add corn and cook till tender. Add a cup of small shrimp and cook till pink. River shrimp are hard to find now, but delicious if you can get them. Add a dash of Worcestershire Sauce, cider vinegar and a teaspoon of sugar while shrimp are cooking. This is such a delicious, simple, and easy soup that is very light, so it is great for a hot day when your tummy doesn't feel like taking on anything too heavy. (Canned shrimp and canned creamed corn may be substituted.)

STUFFED YELLOW SQUASH

Cut tender yellow squash in half. Boil until just tender, or cover and put in microwave for 3 or 4 minutes. Scoop out insides. Chop pulp, and chop small onion finely and shred some ham. Sauté onion and ham in a small skillet, add pulp, and season with tarragon, salt and pepper. When well cooked and blended, mix with a small amount of seasoned bread crumbs. Quantities depend on size of squash. Top with bread crumbs and melted butter and bake until lightly browned. This recipe can also be used with shrimp or crabmeat.

(Author's Recipes)

CAJUN CATFISH

Season eight catfish fillets with salt and cayenne pepper, but not too heavily. Dredge lightly in flour. Chop 1/2 tomato in small pieces and drain off juice. Put a half stick of butter in the pan, and when simmering, but not browning, place the fillets in the pan and broil quickly on each side until lightly browned. Remove and add finely chopped onions to the butter. When onions are soft, add the chopped tomato and simmer until soft. Put the fillets back in the sauce, add a little lemon juice, a dash of Worcestershire sauce, and sprinkle with chopped parsley. The tomato bits are meant to be a subtle addition, and not a tomato sauce.

BROCCOLI, RICE AND CHEESE CASSEROLE

1 cup water	1 pint half and half
2 pkg. chopped frozen broccoli	2 cups cooked rice
1 pkg. frozen diced onions	1 pkg. herb stuffing
2 small cans sliced mushrooms	Salt, lemon pepper to taste
	1 pkg. shredded cheddar cheese
3 pkg. instant creamy onion soup	1/2 pkg. **finely** shredded cheese
	Seasoned bread crumbs

Heat water in large frying pan. When boiling, add vegetables. Simmer until broccoli is tender and add soup mix and half and half. Turn heat off and add cooked rice, herb stuffing, seasoning and mix. Add shredded cheddar cheese and mix well. Place in casserole and sprinkle the finely shredded cheese over the top. Top that with seasoned bread crumbs and pats of butter or melted butter or margarine. Bake for one hour at 350° or until heated through, preferable in a convection oven so that top won't burn.

Grits and Grillades ...

One of the greatest stick-to-your-ribs dishes is grits and grillades, a simple but spicy combination of pieces of young beef rounds cooked in a rich dark gravy and served on a plateful of steaming hot, white Grits. The gravy is sometimes served brown and sometimes as a tomato gravy. Grits, of course, are coarsely ground corn, and in spite of grits being the brunt of many jokes, Southerners continue to prefer them. These Grillades with a dark, rich Tomato Gravy are served with Cheese Grits; Butter Beans with Bacon; Individual Pecan Pies; a Summer Salad of Mandarin Orange Sections, Pineapple Chunks, and Avocado Slices; and a pottery bowl of Croissants. A basket of azaleas with a country blue duck brightens the table.

GRILLADES

Grillades (pronounced gree-yads) are served with grits for breakfast and may be served with either rice or grits for a nice supper dish. Customarily, brown gravy is served with grits and tomato gravy with rice, but it can be served either way.

Separate a heavy veal round into individual steaks, brown well in 2 tablespoons shortening, and remove. Brown 2 tablespoons flour in the same fat until dark brown. Add 1/2 cup of chopped onions, 3 tablespoons each of chopped bell pepper and parsley, and one crushed clove of garlic. Add water gradually until gravy is creamy. Season with salt, pepper, basil and hot sauce; return meat to pot, and simmer for an hour or more. 1 can of tomato sauce (and a can of stewed tomatoes if you wish) may be added to the gravy while it cooks.

HOW TO COOK GRITS

Add 2 tablespoons butter and 1 teaspoon salt to 5 cups boiling water. Slowly stir in 1 cup of white hominy grits. Cover and cook slowly for at least 30 minutes, stirring frequently. You may use instant grits if you wish. They are richer and tastier if cooked with milk and butter instead of water.

CHEESE GRITS

To make cheese grits, add 1 1/2 cups of grated sharp cheese as soon as the grits are removed from the stove and before they start to cool. Stir in a stick of butter and add three beaten eggs. Bake at 300° for about an hour.

(Author's Recipes)

... at a Dogtrot House

A Dogtrot house is probably more commonly found in North Louisiana, although some do occur in South Louisiana. Architecturally, it is the forerunner of a house with a breezeway. In hot weather, the family sat in the shade of the opening between the two sides of the house, and was cooled by the breezes that were drawn through this area. Usually the dogs and cats also found it a pleasant place to lie.

Dogtrot House

BUTTER BEANS WITH BACON

Chop one small onion finely. Cut about four strips of bacon into small pieces. Fry the bacon, drain off most of the grease, and add the onions. Sauté onions until soft and yellow. Put a tablespoon of flour into a small bowl, gradually stirring in 1/2 cup of water and 1/2 cup milk. Pour this mixture into a pot and place over low heat. Add two packages of butter beans or baby limas (or equal amount of fresh beans). Add onion and bacon mixture. Add 1/2 teaspoon of tarragon, one tablespoons of Pickapeppa Sauce, some Worcestershire Sauce and salt to taste. Cook slowly until beans are tender, **adding milk as needed.**

DIVINITY

3 cups sugar	2 egg whites
1/2 cup water	1 teaspoon almond extract
3/4 cup white corn syrup	1 cup chopped nutmeats

Boil sugar, water and corn syrup until it threads. Pour over egg whites which have been beaten until stiff. Toward the end, beat vigorously by hand until it becomes difficult to continue. Add nuts and almond flavor and drop by the spoonful on wax paper.

PECAN PIE

5 egg yolks	1 cup broken pecan meats
1 cup sugar	5 egg whites, well beaten
1 cup white Karo syrup	Vanilla to taste
3 tablespoons margarine	

Cream margarine, sugar and egg yolks. Add syrup, vanilla and pecans and stir well. Fold in egg whites. Pour mixture into unbaked pastry shell and bake slowly at 325° for one hour until custard like in consistency. Serve with ice cream and a few pecans sprinkled over the top, or whipped cream. For whole or individual pies.

PIE CRUST

2 cups flour	1/3 cup white vegetable
1/2 teaspoon salt	shortening
1/3 cup margarine or oleo	Ice water (about 1/3 cup)

Mix salt into flour. Work both shortenings into flour with pastry mixer or by crossing two knives against each other. Bits of shortening should be reduced to pea size. Moisten dough with ice water by stirring with a fork. Pat into 2 balls (for 2 crusts), wrap in wax paper, and chill thoroughly. This dough handles easily and bakes very well.

CHOCOLATE PRALINES
(Please pronounce "prah-leens", not "pray-leens")

2 cups white sugar	3 squares dark chocolate
Pinch of salt	2 cups broken pecan meats
1 cup half and half	1 teaspoon vanilla
1 cup brown sugar	2 tablespoon butter

Boil white sugar, cream and salt to softball stage (235°), stirring occasionally. Meanwhile, melt chocolate in a double boiler and when main recipe is ready, melt brown sugar in a heavy bottomed pan. (Don't scorch). Add melted sugar and chocolate and pecan pieces. Cook a minute or two longer, remove from heat, add vanilla and beat well. Spoon onto buttered surface, making them small or large, as you prefer.

SUMMER SALAD

Line a large bowl or individual bowls with separated leaves of lettuce. Drain two cans of mandarin orange sections, one large can of pineapple chunks, one can of grapefruit sections, and slice one or two avocados. Sprinkle the avocado slices with lemon juice, mix with fruit and add poppy seed dressing. Serve in lettuce lined bowls.

What in the World is a Pigeonnier? ...

If you have not caught the sound of it, we explain that a pigeonnier is a place where pigeons are kept. We think of dove cotes and squab as being associated more with the wealthy Creoles, but the Acadians kept pigeons too, although they were more apt to have just an entry loft for the pigeons in the top of the chicken house. Almost everything on the face of the earth that flew, or ran, or swam was fair game for the stock pot. Poule d' eau, (water chicken or coot) was even allowed on Fridays because it ate only "water things" and tasted rather more like fish than fowl. It was usually used in a gumbo.

Pigeonnier (Dove Cote)

"DIRTY" RICE

The name "dirty rice" is a local joke among Acadian people and comes from the look of the rice when served. After all the meat, giblets, and seasonings are mixed in, it is quite dark and looks as if it has been well dirtied up.

1/2 to 1 pound chicken giblets which have been boiled until tender	1/4 cup chopped parsley
	2 cloves of crushed garlic
	Salt and black or red pepper
1 pound ground chuck	1/4 cup chopped green onion tops
1 cup chopped onions	
1/2 cup bell pepper	Pinch of thyme or basil
1/2 cup chopped celery	2 cups rice

Sauté ground meat and ground or chopped giblets in 1/4 cup bacon drippings until brown. Drain off excess fat, add seasonings and continue to cook a few minutes. While simmering the meat and seasonings, the rice can be cooking. It will have more flavor if it is cooked in 4 cups of chicken stock or giblet liquid for 18 minutes. Drain rice and mix thoroughly into the meat mixture. Spoon into a greased casserole and bake at 300° for 20 to 30 minutes until dry. Some cooks prefer to continue the cooking in a heavy pot on top of the stove, but great care must be taken not to let it burn at the bottom.

(Author's Recipes)

BRUSSELS SPROUTS EN CASSEROLE

Cook fresh or frozen Brussels Sprouts until tender. Stir one cup or more of chicken broth into one tablespoon or more of flour, depending on how many sprouts you are cooking. Add salt, pepper and 1/2 teaspoon of tarragon, and simmer in a separate pot until it has cooked down somewhat. Add sprouts and continue cooking until they are coated with the sauce.

COUNTRY BISCUITS

2 1/2 cups plain flour	1 1/2 tablespoons baking
1/2 teaspoon salt	powder
	3 tablespoons sugar

Mix flour, salt, sugar and baking powder all together very well. Cut in 3/4 cup Crisco. Add enough milk to hold dough together— about 2/3 cup. Put mixture on floured board, knead a couple of times, and roll to 3/4" thickness. Cut with a 2" cutter and place on ungreased pan. Bake in preheated 450° oven for approximately 20 minutes or until golden brown. Makes 15 biscuits.

CAJUN FRIED CHICKEN

Cut fryer into pieces of desired size. Sprinkle liberally with salt and lemon pepper. Add 1/2 teaspoon each of salt and cayenne (red) pepper—or more if desired—to one cup of flour in a brown paper bag. Shake the pieces in the bag and remove. Place the covered chicken in the refrigerator for a couple of hours to give the seasoning time to take effect. Cook in deep fat at 375°. Cajuns float a match on top of the heating oil, and when it lights, that means the grease is hot enough. I have never been brave enough to try it, but it works for them. Remove each piece when it is golden brown. Small pieces fry faster. Some Acadians prefer to make a batter with buttermilk and flour and dip the chicken in it and then in flour, but remember that no respectable Cajun would forget to season with plenty of cayenne pepper.

HOT POTATO SALAD

1 onion, coarsely chopped	2 cooked potatoes, sliced
1 bell pepper, cut in strips	6 slices bacon, cooked and
2 tablespoons olive oil	cut into one inch slices
2 tablespoons vinegar	1 teaspoon basil
2 tablespoons sugar	Salt and black or red pepper

Sauté onion and pepper in olive oil until soft. Add vinegar and sugar. Add potato slices and bacon pieces. Add seasoning as you gently stir and heat thoroughly. Pimento may also be added for color. You may want to add some of the vinegar and sugar slowly as you cook everything together and check for taste.

... and What is a Juchoir?

The Juchoir, or chicken roost, was as much an integral part of an Acadian farm as the pigeonnier was to the grand antebellum mansions. Juchoirs were as practical as they were clever looking. The hens climbed up their tiny ladders at night, and when mama hen hatched out biddies, they could be kept safe here from foxes and possums. Fried Chicken in this swampy country was hot with pepper and "Dirty Rice" was the traditional accompaniment. Even today, at locally owned fast food chicken restaurants, the chicken is served with Dirty Rice. People of Acadian descent expect it to be served that way. Potato Salad was also a traditional accompaniment. You will notice that Cajuns had no qualms about balanced meals and more than one starch at a meal. Here at our little chicken roost, we have Country Fried Chicken; Hot Potato Salad with Red and Green Bell Pepper Chunks; Dirty Rice; Brussels Sprouts en Casserole; and Biscuits with Cane Syrup.

Mais Cher, Sugar House Parties Were the Best ...

In French country, sentences often start with "Mais, Cher" ..., (but my dear ...,"). In the early part of the century, one of the favorite places to have a party in the fall of the year was at an "open kettle" sugar house. A "sugar house" is where the cane is ground to a mashed pulp in order to extract the juice. "Grinding" lasts from October to January. The juice is boiled to the consistency of a syrup, which goes through several stages until sugar is produced. The kind of heavy syrup that you can almost eat with a fork was called La Cuite, and is still sold by a few companies. Alcohol is a by-product of sugar, and sometimes, when the syrup was just fresh, there was still a trace of the alcohol. They loved to mix whole fresh pecans with the La Cuite and eat it, and a by-product of that performance was sometimes to get a little tipsy. "Cuite" means baked, but in French slang also means drunk. Needless to say, the parties were not as fancy as in our picture, and did not use Grandmere's best Moss Rose porcelain.

Old Open Kettle Sugar House

ANISE COOKIES

These are the very favorite cookies of the Acadian people, especially at Christmas time. The word is pronounced ah-neese here in Acadiana.

3/4 cup sugar	2 cups flour
1/2 cup butter or margarine	1/2 teaspoon baking powder
2 eggs	(double acting)
4 drops oil of anise	1/4 teaspoon salt

Cream sugar into butter thoroughly. Stir eggs and anise oil into it and beat well. Sift flour with baking powder and salt, and stir into other ingredients. When well blended, shape dough into walnut sized balls. Bake on a greased cookie sheet, leaving a couple of inches between the balls, at 350°. Do not brown. Usually varicolored, tiny candy granulates are pressed into the top of the cookies just before baking. Should make about 3 dozen cookies.

(Author's Recipes)

AUNT DELLA'S TEA CAKE RECIPE

4 cups flour	1 1/2 cups butter, softened
1 teaspoon soda	1/2 cup buttermilk
1/2 teaspoon salt	2 eggs, beaten
1 1/2 cups sugar	1 teaspoon vanilla and coconut flavoring

Sift dry ingredients together. Cut shortening (butter, margarine, or butter flavored Crisco) into dry ingredients with a pastry cutter or two crossed knives until the particles are as fine as corn meal. Beat the eggs into the buttermilk and pour into the flour mixture. Stir well and chill. Roll out to about 1/4 inch thick and cut out with a cookie cutter. Sprinkle sugar over the top. Place on a greased cookie sheet and bake at 350° till golden. Cookies will be crispy.

(from Dot Bergeron)

JELLY ROLL

Use standard roll cake pan—10 1/2 x 15 1/2 with a 1 inch rim all around. Grease with vegetable oil or baking spray.

4 eggs, separated	1/3 cup cornstarch
1 teaspoon almond extract	1/2 cup cake flour
(or vanilla)	Raspberry jam, or any jelly
1/4 teaspoon salt	or jam you prefer
1/2 cup granulated sugar	Confectioners' sugar

Beat egg whites, adding salt when foamy , and beat until they form peaks. Add sugar, little by little, and continue beating, but stop before they get too stiff and dry. Beat yolks and add almond extract. Gently pour yolks into whites, and carefully fold them in until blended. Now fold in flour and cornstarch . Line pan with wax paper, and spread mixture in the pan. Bake at 350° for 15 minutes or longer, until a toothpick comes out clean. Dust confectioners' sugar over wax paper or a kitchen towel and carefully turn the jelly roll pan upside down. Remove the wax paper and trim sides. Roll cake in the towel from side to side (not lengthwise) and cool. When cold, unroll, beat jelly so it will handle easily and carefully spread it on the cake. Roll up again, leaving towel behind, and dust top with confectioners' sugar.

BANANA MARSHMALLOW ROLL

Use Jelly Roll recipe above. Soften a jar of marshmallow cream according to directions on jar. Mash at least two bananas and spread on cooled jelly roll. Spread marshmallow cream on top of bananas and roll up. Dust with confectioners' sugar and chill thoroughly.

... and Nothin' Tastes Better than Open Kettle Syrup Made from Ribbon Cane.

The new sugar houses have large pressurized copper tanks in which to boil the sugar. The sugar boilers are the prima donnas of the sugar house, because they have to know when the syrup is at the right stage to drop into the centrifuges on the floor below, in order to spin it into dry sugar. They watch the bubbles through a small glass window and periodically take out a small sample of the syrup to test for sugar crystals. Now, they even have computerization in the sugar house. How sad! It misses the excitement and danger of an old open kettle sugar house, when everything was based on skill and judgement.

Ribbon cane is a soft, white-striped cane, which is not disease resistant. Many still grow a patch of it, in order to have a small amount of the sweet old-fashioned syrup. At this party fancy things are displayed, such as Banana Marshmallow Roll, Jelly Roll, Lemon Pound Cake, Apple Muffins, Miniature Biscuits with Cane Syrup, Creamy Pralines, Large Macaroons, Anise Cookies topped with Colored Candy Sprinkles, Brownies with Chopped Pecans, Roasted Pecan Halves, and Candy Coated Licorice Pastilles.

LEMON POUND CAKE

3 1/2 cups cake flour	2 1/3 cups superfine sugar
1 teaspoon baking powder	8 eggs, unbeaten
1/8 teaspoon salt	1 teaspoon pure vanilla
1 3/4 cups butter	2 ounces lemon extract

Sift flour once and measure. Add baking powder and salt. Sift together three times. Cream butter thoroughly, add sugar gradually, and cream together until light and fluffy. Add eggs one at a time, beating several minutes after each addition. Add flour a small amount at a time, beating after each addition. Add flavoring and beat vigorously for several minutes. Bake in two paper lined loaf pans at 300° for 40 minutes. Then increase heat to 325° and bake for 1 hour and 20 minutes.

MACAROONS

1/2 pound almond paste	2 tablespoons pastry flour
1 cup sugar	1/3 cup powdered sugar
3 egg whites	

Mix paste by hand, adding sugar and egg whites slowly, and blend thoroughly. Sift powdered sugar with flour into mixture and finish blending. Still using hands, form into balls the size of a nutmeg, and lay on cookie sheet which has been covered with wax paper. Keep one inch apart. Cover and let stand overnight. Dip your fingers in cold water and gently pat tops of cookies. Bake 25 minutes in 300° oven until very lightly browned. Cool a little while and turn upside down. Wring out a piece of cloth that has been dipped in cold water. Wet back of paper and remove cookies.

That's Where the Cotton and the Corn and Taters Grow.

Cotton and Corn are both big crops in Louisiana. Cotton has mostly moved to the northern part of the state. Corn is grown everywhere, and used in every way, as you will see throughout this cookbook. Here we have "punkins" instead of "taters". Pumpkin bread and pumpkin soup are popular in Louisiana, as well as pumpkin pie. Our luncheon spread includes Stuffed Bell Peppers, French Style Green Beans, Macaroni and Cheese, Cocounut Custard Pie, and (always) Red Wine. Many of the planters always had a **tumbler** *of red wine for lunch.*

Brick and Timber Shed, called "Brique entre Poteaux" construction, meaning Brick between Posts.

STUFFED BELL PEPPERS

6 green bell peppers
1 tomato, chopped
1 rib celery, chopped
1 onion, chopped
2 tablespoons butter
1 tablespoon bacon fat
1 cup cooked rice

2 cups cooked meat
   or seafood
1 egg
1/4 cup crumbled bacon
Salt and pepper to taste
Water or bouillon

Remove tops from peppers, take out seeds, wash and parboil for just a few minutes. Sauté chopped vegetables in butter and bacon fat. Mix together rice, meat, vegetables, beaten egg and seasoning. Add water or bouillon as needed to season. Fill peppers with rice mixture, sprinkle bread crumbs and parmesan cheese on top, and dot with butter. Bake in buttered baking dish with a little water in the bottom at 350° until browned. Tomato sauce may be used in baking dish instead of water, to be used as a sauce with the peppers.

FLUFFY COCONUT CUSTARD PIE

5 eggs, beaten
1 stick butter or margarine
3/4 cup buttermilk

2 cups sugar
2 cups shredded coconut
1 unbaked pie shell (9″)

Mix all ingredients well. Beat really hard. Pour into pie shell and bake at 350° about 30 minutes or until pie is done. Makes a very thick and fluffy pie.

(from Dorothy Daniels)

CAJUN MACARONI AND CHEESE

1 regular package of elbow
   or small shell macaroni
1 cup shredded cheddar
   cheese
2 tablespoons butter
1/2 cup chopped green onion

1/2 cup chopped green
   pepper
1 can evaporated milk
2 eggs, beaten
1 teaspoon mustard
Salt and pepper to taste

Cook macaroni and drain. While macaroni is cooking, sauté vegetables. While macaroni is still hot, add cheese and mix in well to make it melt a little. Beat eggs into milk and pour into macaroni. Add sautéed vegetables and mix again. Pour into buttered baking dish. Top with seasoned bread crumbs and dots of butter if you wish. Bake until bubbly and crusty. Everyone loves to scrape out the "gratins" (pronounced grah - tans') and eat them. This refers to the crunchy browned portion which adheres around the sides of the baking dish.

FRENCH STYLE GREEN BEANS

Enough fresh, frozen, or
   canned french cut green
   beans to serve four people
   (Equivalent of two packages)
1 tablespoon cooking oil

1 tablespoon flour
2 strips of bacon, chopped
1 tablespoon Worcestershire
   sauce
Salt and cayenne pepper
   to taste

Sauté onion in oil in frying pan until soft. Add flour and brown. Add a small amount of water and beans, and keep adding water as necessary. Add bacon, Worcestershire sauce and seasonings. Cook until very well done.

(Author's Recipes)

13

"Po' Boys," a Meal in a Loaf

Almost no self-respecting South Louisiana family is without French Bread, unless they are displaced Yankees. It is used for everything, including Turkey Stuffing, Bread Pudding, Bread Crumbs, and Pain Perdu or Lost Bread, (French Toast, which is made with stale bread). A "Po' Boy" was so called because it was the cheapest lunch possible—just a huge sandwich of French bread which could be copiously filled with anything from ham and cheese or chicken, to meat balls or fried oysters. They are not so cheap today, but they have always been consumed by rich and poor alike. One can be inventive, for the possibilities are endless. One of these is filled with Ham and Cheddar Cheese and the other with Turkey and Baby Swiss Cheese, and are served simply, with Potato Chips, Bread and Butter Pickles, and a Bowl of Mandarin Oranges. Coffee is often served in a glass, with the spoon in it, to stir a copious amount of sugar, until the strong coffee, which may have chicory in it, begins to taste like syrup.

COLD PO' BOYS

A "Po' Boy" sandwich is made up of an entire small loaf of French Bread, or about 1/4 of one of the extremely long loaves of French bread, sliced lengthwise into a top and bottom. It is then spread with mayonnaise, butter or any other spread and topped with mustard (preferably hot), ketchup or any other dressing or sauce that seems to go well with the contents. Restaurants always ask if you want your Po' Boy "dressed" which means with mayonnaise, lettuce, and tomatoes, or any other condiment you desire. You then lay your preference of meat and cheese along the length of the loaf, add pickles if you wish, and close it up. Then you can cut the loaf into shorter sandwiches suitable for everyone. Another option is to buy the smaller individual loaves and make one up for each person. One rich and tasty combination is to put ham and roast beef together in the same sandwich. Cold shrimp or crabmeat salad make a fantastic filling. Salami, bologna, pastrami, and corned beef are all excellent "stuffings" and two kinds of cheese can be added to any of the above. Use your imagination.

HOT PO' BOYS

Cold Po' Boys are wonderful in hot weather, but hot Po' Boys are equally wonderful in cold weather. Some restaurants cut off one end of a Po' Boy loaf, pull out the inside of the bread, and then fill it with small meatballs in a tomato or barbecue sauce. You eat it tipped up on end, to save your tie. Fried oysters, shrimp, crawfish and catfish are all equally suitable stuffings. Add ketchup, hot sauce, or tartar sauce as you wish. Hot roast meats of any kind, with gravy are fine. On one occasion I was given a delicious lamb sandwich (hot or cold) with lettuce and mint jelly. Even fried eggs and bacon can be found layered between pieces of French Bread. So go do your own thing. One of the greatest hot sandwiches that can be had is a hot crab or shrimp loaf. Just make a hot crab or shrimp dip with a cream sauce thick enough so that it doesn't slide out of the sandwich.

Lazy Bayou

Bayou Country ... It Puts Your Soul at Peace.

There is something very peaceful about sitting beside a bayou and watching the water, which seems to be in no hurry to get anywhere. If one sits quietly and unobtrusively among the cover of some nearby cypress trees, there is no end to what can be seen. A heron walking in slow motion, lifting his feet carefully so as not to disturb the water, but with his beak aimed straight down, ready to grab anything that looks like a meal. Or perhaps a raccoon, patting his paws in the shallow water along the edge, feeling for succulent crawfish. Sometimes an otter plays like an energetic child, diving and circling as if in a dance, and then comes up with a fish in his forepaws, and eats it like an ice cream cone.

HOW TO MAKE CAJUN COFFEE

One cannot duplicate "Cajun" Coffee without a true French drip coffee pot, usually of white enamel. The coffee used is dark roast ground coffee. A blend with chicory may be used, but plain dark roast is more commonly used by Acadians. Use 2 table- spoons of coffee for each cup of water. Any amount of a lighter roast coffee will not taste the same. Adding more coffee to make it stronger just doesn't do the trick.

Boil the water and drip it slowly, about 1 tablespoonful at a time, through the coffee that is in the top part of the pot. The pot must be kept hot while the water is dripping, so it is set in a pot of boiling water on the stove. Always reheat the coffee with the pot set in another pan of water, not directly on the heat. One old French- man, referring to the minute amount of water added at a time, commented, "Oh, they just walk by and spit in it every now and then."

This coffee will grow hair on your chest, I "gah - rahn - tee"!

(Author's Recipes)

PAIN ORDINAIRE
("Common" French Bread)

Dissolve an envelope of yeast in 1/4 cup warm water. Add 1 1/2 teaspoons salt, 1 3/4 cups lukewarm water and stir in softened yeast. Slowly stir in 5 cups regular flour. Turn onto floured board and knead 10 minutes till dough becomes smooth and elastic.

Let covered dough rise in a greased bowl until bulk is doubled (about 2 hours). See if finger leaves an indentation that remains. Punch dough down until it doubles again. Turn onto floured board and knead lightly.

Shape dough into 2 long loaves. Let rise on a greased baking sheet (covered) in a warm place until double in size. When half risen, cut diagonal slits a few times across the top. Brush surface with milk and bake in a 400° oven for 50 minutes until golden. A pan of boiling water on the bottom of the oven will produce a heavier crust on the bread.

15

If You Don't Have a Watch Dog ... Get a Goose!

Acadian people like their geese. Geese proudly walk around the yard, talking to each other, and always sound a warning when a stranger approaches. If no one is there to do something about it, they don't mind attacking one bit. If the gaggle of geese gets too large, roast goose is always one answer to culling the flock.

RED SNAPPER COURTBOUILLON

1/4 cup toasted bread cubes	1/2 cup crabmeat
4 tablespoons butter	1/4 cup white wine
6 chopped green onions	1/2 cup mushrooms, chopped
1 stalk celery, chopped	1/2 teaspoon basil
1 tablespoon chopped parsley	Salt and pepper to taste

Moisten bread cubes with a little boiling water and mix well with the melted butter in which all the chopped vegetables have been sautéed; include the seasonings, and the crabmeat and wine. Place cleaned fish in a baking dish. Head is usually left on. Rub outside of fish with butter and season with salt and pepper. Stuff fish and fasten cavity closed. Pour the Courtbouillon Sauce around it in the dish. Poach in the sauce for about 30 minutes, in a 350° oven. Baste occasionally with the juice, adding more liquid as needed. Red wine may also be added to the sauce. (Some chefs prefer to bake fillets in the Courtbouillon, rather than the whole fish.)

BLACK BEAN SOUP

1 pound black beans	1/2 cup chopped parsley
2 cups sausage, cut 1/4" thick	Salt, garlic salt, lemon pepper
1/2 cup chopped green onions	Oil of anise, or anisette to taste

Wash beans well, then cover with enough water and soak overnight. Cook for a long time until beans are tender. About halfway through the cooking time, add the sausage (which has been fried and drained), onions, and seasonings. If you can find Italian Sausage, it already has the anise flavoring and you will not have to add it. Add water as necessary, keeping it the consistency of soup. Near the end, add the parsley. Before serving, add a pat of butter to each bowl and float thin slices of lemon on top of the soup, sprinkled with paprika.

(Author's Recipes)

COURTBOUILLON SAUCE

1 can tomatoes, chopped	1/2 teaspoon basil
2 onions, diced	1 small can mushrooms
2 stalks celery, chopped	1/4 cup chopped parsley
1 bell pepper, diced	Salt, lemon pepper, and
1 small can V-8 juice	cayenne pepper to taste

This is a poaching medium, used in the same way as a clear courtbouillon, except that it is richer and a little thicker, but keep it light enough so that it doesn't overwhelm the fish. Cook tomatoes, add vegetables, salt and pepper and continue cooking until tender. Add V-8 juice while cooking, and water as necessary. Add the mushrooms and parsley just before finishing. This sauce can also be used with fish fillets.

COUNTRY CORN PUDDING

4 cups cut corn	Seasoned bread crumbs
4 eggs	1 stick butter
1 tablespoon diced pimento	Salt and cayenne pepper
2 tablespoons diced bell	to taste
pepper	Paprika

Cut corn from fresh cob and then scrape and catch "milk" until you have four cups of corn and liquid. Canned cream style corn or whole kernel corn, or a combination of the two may be substituted. Beat eggs with a fork and add to corn with the pimento and bell pepper. Spread 1/3 of this mixture over the bottom of a deep casserole. Sprinkle a layer of bread crumbs over this, and dot with pats of butter. Repeat this procedure twice, but stop before you add the bread crumbs the last time. Slowly pour the milk over the dish, then add the bread crumbs and butter, and sprinkle with paprika. Bake at 350° until firm.

Pair of Geese

A Good Red Courtbouillon on a Fresh Caught Red Snapper ... Ah, ... C'est Si Bon!

Yes, that's so good! The Parisian French chefs make a white Courtbouillion to simmer fish in, but the Cajuns almost always make a fairly thick tomato Courtbouillon, and either poach or bake the fish in it. Here the whole Red Snapper has been baked, and is accompanied by Black Bean Soup with Anise Flavored Sausage and Thin Lemon Slices; Corn Pudding; Chopped Cucumber and Green Onion Salad; and Peach Shortcake made with Sugared Biscuits. The fish can also be cut into fillets or chunks, if you prefer not to deal with the whole fish.

OLD FASHIONED PEACH SHORTCAKE

2 cups flour	1/3 cup butter
2 teaspoons baking powder	1/3 cup milk
1/2 teaspoon salt	1 egg or 2 egg yolks
1/4 cup sugar	

Mix flour, double acting baking powder, salt and sugar. Sift together twice and then work in butter with a pastry mixer or with two knives, crossing against each other. Add the milk slowly, but stop when you get it to the proper consistency to roll out and handle. Divide, and roll out on floured board in two parts. Put one part in a greased square or oblong tin or baking dish. Drizzle melted butter over it, and put the other half on top. Bake 12 minutes in a hot oven. This can also be made in biscuit shapes, one on top of another buttered shape, and baked on a greased cookie sheet.

Split with a fork, butter, and spread fresh or frozen peaches or strawberries between and on top. Serve with whipping cream or heavy cream.

CUCUMBER AND GREEN ONION SALAD

Peel two cucumbers, quarter, and slice thinly, or chop in very small chunks. Cut up green onions, using some of the tops. Chop some mint and add to the mixture. Now fold in sour cream and mix until everything is thoroughly coated. Chill well before serving. This is a cooling salad for summertime.

(Author's Recipes)

Whether You're Goin' Fishin' or Comin' from Huntin' ...

Fishing was serious business, because it was to provide the main course for supper, so no one wanted to waste time on fixing food or eating fancy sandwiches. So, ... one just passed by the country store and picked up a roll of Garlic Bologna and a large chunk of Hoop Cheese, or as some call it, Rat Cheese. Then all that had to be done was to take a good strong pocket knife out of the old hip pocket and carve off some slices. Along with a lot of big old Soda Crackers and a six pack, this made a meal and a half. It didn't hurt to have some big Dill Pickles on hand, either.

Sausage and Beans on a Paper Plate

WHITE BEANS AND SAUSAGE

1 pound small white beans	2 bay leaves
1 large onion, chopped	1/4 cup butter or margarine
1/4 cup green onion tops	6 slices bacon, cut in pieces
1/4 cup chopped pimento	Salt and cayenne pepper
1/4 cup chopped parsley	to taste

Wash beans, change water and bring to a rolling boil for a few minutes. Remove from heat and soak overnight in that same water, enough to cover the beans. In the morning, bring to boil again and add everything except the butter. Reduce heat and simmer for 3 hours. Peas should be creamy but remain whole. Add butter and mix well. Serve over hot fluffy rice.

BOUDIN

8 pounds pork meat, cut into pieces small enough to grind	4 cloves garlic
	Salt and cayenne pepper
2 pounds pork liver, cut up	to taste
2 large onions, cut up	4 pounds long grained rice
1 large bell pepper, cut up	Sausage casing and sausage
2 stalks celery, cut in lengths	stuffer

Put meat, vegetables, and seasonings in a big pot and cover with water. Cook on high for at least two hours until meat is tender. Strain off broth and cook until it is reduced to about half the original amount. Meanwhile, grind the meat mixture or process in a food chopper. Mix the meat gently with the rice, adding a little broth as needed, to make it hold together. You may not need all of it. Stuff the mixture into the casing and tie ends.

BREAD AND BUTTER PICKLES

Slice four quarts washed, unpeeled cucumbers thinly. Slice white onions and make thin strips of bell peppers which have been washed and seeded. Mix in a half cup salt and let stand for 4 hours. Rinse repeatedly in cold water and drain well. Add to a hot syrup made of the following, which has been boiled for ten minutes:

4 cups brown sugar	1 tablespoon celery seed
5 cups cider vinegar	Pinch of ground cloves
2 tablespoons mustard seed	2 teaspoons turmeric

Jar and seal.

PEACHES IN BOURBON

Marinate peach halves in bourbon overnight in the refrigerator. Serve in wide sherbet glasses with a touch of nutmeg. This may not sound as elegant as peaches in champagne, but the taste is much more impressive.

MACARONI SALAD

1 cup small shell macaroni	1 tablespoon sweet hot or
1/2 pound cheddar cheese	Creole mustard
1 can English green peas (not petit pois)	1/2 tablespoon vinegar
	1/2 tablespoon sugar
1/4 cup sweet pickle relish with a little juice	1/4 cup each of chopped parsley, shallots and
1/2 cup mayonnaise	pimento
	Salt and pepper to taste

Cook macaroni and cut cheddar cheese into small cubes. Let macaroni cool, because the cheese will be nicer in the salad if it doesn't melt from the hot macaroni. Mix all other ingredients well and chill before serving.

This makes a fine substitute when you have had enough potato salad for awhile and want a change. More vinegar and sugar can be added if you really like a strong sweet and sour taste.

CHERRY BOUNCE

In rural communities, cherry bounce is made with wild cherries, sugar and bourbon. For city folk and those of us who have squirrels and blue jays that beat us to the cherries, a fine substitute may be made as follows:

2 cans or 2 packages frozen black cherries	1 fifth of Southern Comfort

The cherries do not have to be pitted as the seeds add flavor, but if they are pitted, you can use them after you drain off the liqueur to serve over ice cream.

Drain cherries, put in a quart jar with a wide mouth, and cover with Southern Comfort. Since the liqueur and cherries are both sweet, no sugar is needed. Let stand for 2 weeks or longer, then pour off the liqueur. Cherry Bounce is potent, and should be served in small liqueur glasses. A friend of ours used to call this "Cherry Flash", an apt description for the effect.

(Author's Recipes)

... the Country Store Is the Place to Stop.

When coming back from a hunting trip on a freezing cold day, when the water was like ice, it was a welcome sight to come upon a country store that advertised "Hot Boudin". Most of them kept a crock pot full of White Boudin, which is a kind of homemade sausage with rice in it. For a small sum, they would furnish a French Loaf, split in half lengthwise, a paper plate, and a link of Boudin, with perhaps a jar of mustard to dip into. They might even have some White Beans, cooked with onions and bell peppers, in another crock pot. Often, the stores carried Fromage de Tête, which means Head Cheese, but does not have to be made with the meat from the head. It is considered a real delicacy, both in France and in Louisiana, and is usually hotly seasoned.

CAJUN PICKLE RELISH

2 quarts vinegar
1 cup brown sugar
9 bell peppers
6 large onions
1 cabbage

1/4 pound mustard seed
1 teaspoon celery seed
1 teaspoon turmeric
1/2 teaspoon red pepper
Pinch of salt

Heat sugar in vinegar. Chop vegetables in small chunks, not too fine, and soak 12 hours in salted cold water. Drain vegetables and spices well, and add to hot liquid. Bring slowly to a rolling boil. Put in hot, sterilized jars and seal.

Cajun Cookin' Was Invented in the "Pot au Feu".

A famous Chef has said that Cajun Cooking is the only cuisine that was truly invented in America. It was invented out of necessity. A big black stew pot was kept on the back of the stove, and whatever they grew or raised in the yard, or caught in the bayou, or shot in the woods went into it. It was the same "pot au feu" that is used in France and in all peasant cultures, but this was a subtropical environment, and a lot of wonderful vegetables and herbs grew here. More black pans and skillets sat on the front of the stove, and one could panbroil some Garlic Shrimp, or make a dark roux, rich with tomatoes and highly seasoned, and have a marvelous Shrimp Creole to serve over hot fluffy rice. Vegetables were almost always cooked with some kind of meat or seafood.

SHRIMP CREOLE

4 pounds peeled raw shrimp	1 cup water
1/4 cup flour	3 bay leaves
1/4 cup oil or margarine	1 tablespoon sugar
1 cup chopped onions	1 tablespoon Worcestershire
1 cup chopped celery	sauce
1 cup chopped bell pepper	1 tablespoon lemon juice
2 cloves garlic, minced	1/2 cup chopped parsley
1 (6 oz.) can tomato paste	Salt and lemon pepper,
1 (16 oz.) can stewed	cayenne (red pepper), or
tomatoes	tabasco to taste, or any
1 (8 oz.) can tomato sauce	combination thereof

Make a dark brown roux of flour and oil (or bacon grease) in a large heavy pot, adding water very slowly after desired color is achieved. Add vegetables and sauté until soft. Add tomato paste and mix well with vegetables, cooking until it almost turns color. Add all other ingredients except the shrimp and parsley. Simmer slowly for one hour, covered, stirring occasionally. Add shrimp and cook until done, 5 minutes or more, depending on size. Add parsley at the same time. Serve over hot rice. (Tastes even better on the next day.)

**Recipe from Cookin' Cajun
Cooking School in New Orleans**

Shrimp Creole

PAN BROILED GARLIC SHRIMP

24 large shrimp	1 teaspoon bouquet garni
1/2 stick butter	1 tablespoon brown sugar
1 onion, diced	1 tablespoon Worcestershire
6 cloves garlic, minced	sauce
2 slices bacon, minced	2 tablespoons lemon juice
3 tablespoons white wine	Salt and cayenne pepper
2 tablespoons teriyaki sauce	to taste

Melt butter in a large sauté pan. Add onions, garlic and bacon and sauté till lightly browned. Fry bits of bacon separately and drain off fat. Add all remaining ingredients and simmer for 5 more minutes. Add shrimp and cook just until pink and tender. Do not overcook.

SHRIMP AND TRI-COLOR FUSILLI

Sauté 1/2 cup each of onion, green bell pepper, and celery, finely chopped in 2 tablespoons of olive oil. Cut the following in large chunks:

1 red and 1 yellow bell pepper	1 small zucchini
1 green tomato (or red)	1 small yellow squash

Add to pan and stir fry. Don't overcook. Add at least 2 tablespoons of White Worcestershire Sauce, salt and lemon pepper to taste. Then add a pound of medium size shrimp and 1 cup tricolor fuselli (plain, carrot, and spinach), both of which have been cooked ahead of time. Add a little white wine, heat through and serve.

(Author's Recipes)

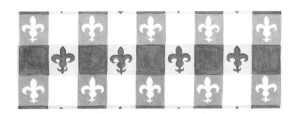

Pan Broiled Garlic Shrimp

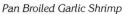

21

We Assembled a "Stuffed Supper" of Cajun Delicacies.

The Stuffed Supper title is our own invention (not Cajun), but so many of the delicious Cajun dishes involve the stuffing of something or other. In our little kitchen corner, the crabmeat has been removed from the crab shells, mixed with onions, seasoning and herbed rice and stuffed back in. Viola! Stuffed Crabs. The stuffed Potatoes have been similarly emptied and mashed with cheddar cheese, and chopped green onions, and refilled. The Stuffed Mirlitons are flavored with River Shrimp. Mirlitons are sometimes called Vegetable Pears or Chayote. Their flavor is very delicate, and so are the river shrimp, ... a made in heaven combination.

STUFFED CRABS

2 cups lump crabmeat	1 cup bread crumbs
1 finely chopped onion	2 eggs, beaten
1/4 cup chopped celery	1 pint half and half
1/4 cup chopped parsley	2 tablespoons ketchup
1/2 cup butter	Salt and cayenne pepper
1/4 teaspoon thyme	to taste

Sauté onions, parsley, and celery in butter until soft and add crabmeat. Mix thyme in, then bread crumbs and beaten eggs, and toss with a fork. Add cream until mixture has the right degree of moisture, and blend in the ketchup, which gives it just a subtle touch of tomato. Add salt and cayenne (red) pepper to suit your taste. Fill eight cleaned or ceramic crab shells and bake at 350° for 15 minutes or until golden brown.

STUFFED MIRLITONS WITH SHRIMP

4 mirlitons	2 bay leaves
4 green onions	1 tablespoon chopped parsley
1 stick butter or margarine	1 cup bread crumbs
1 pound small shrimp	Salt and white pepper
(cleaned)	Paprika

The most important thing to remember about preparing mirlitons is their deliciously delicate flavor. No matter what meat or seafood you use, don't smother the taste with strong seasonings. Cut the mirlitons in half and remove the seed. Place in a microwave, cover with a paper towel, and cook at full power in increments of 3 minutes until pulp is tender (or parboil in water). Scoop out pulp and save the shell. Chop pulp up so that there are no lumps. Finely chop green onions, including some of the tender tops, and sauté in butter. Add mirliton pulp and bay leaves and continue cooking until everything is well cooked. Add parsley and shrimp and cook until shrimp are pink. Remove bay leaves and season to taste. Stuff mirliton shells, sprinkle tops with bread crumbs and paprika, drizzle butter over the top and bake at 350° for 20 minutes.

22

Food is the Main Topic of Conversation in Louisiana

The scent of the huge blossoms of Magnolia gradiflora, which are the size of dinner plates, is heavenly. But there is nothing so heavenly as the scents that come from the kitchen of an Acadian family. No puny boiled food for them; no unseasoned food; and no worries about cooking food to death. The more one cooks it, the more the flavor blends. It is not unusual to cut up an eggplant, boil it, drain it, then fry it with onions, oil, tomatoes, and meat, and finish it up by baking it with breadcrumbs. Believe it, no eggplant ever tasted so good. Recipes are exchanged more by word of mouth than by cookbooks.

BREAD PUDDING WITH AMARETTO SAUCE

1 loaf stale French Bread
1 quart milk
1/2 cup sugar
6 eggs
1 cup raisins
1 tablespoon vanilla
Splash of Amaretto (add to hot bread pudding)

In a large bowl, soak bread in milk. Add sugar, raisins, and vanilla. Add eggs. Mix very lightly. Place in well-buttered baking dish. Bake at 375° for 30 to 45 minutes. Serves 8.

AMARETTO SAUCE

1 stick unsalted butter
1 cup powdered sugar
1/4 cup Amaretto
1 egg yolk

Over low heat, melt butter and sugar together, stirring constantly. Add Amaretto and egg yolk. Heat slowly for one or two minutes to set eggs. Poke holes in bread pudding and pour sauce over it.

Recipe from Cookin' Cajun Cooking School in New Orleans

STEAMED CABBAGE WEDGES WITH HAM SLICES

Cut head of cabbage in wedges, arrange carefully in a basket that you can suspend over a pot of water, or in a steamer, and steam until tender but not too soft, so that the wedges will hold their shape. Arrange with heated thick slices of ham between them on a platter. Serve with salt, pepper, vinegar and mustard on the table so that each person can season his own serving.

FIELD PEAS AND SNAPS

If you are lucky enough to get young, fresh field peas, you will probably find that there will be slender green pods among them that do not have mature beans in them. Just snap these and add them to the pot. Cook as you do other beans, but add a light roux and some chopped onions like the Cajuns do. Very tasty! If you don't have the real thing, you can mix some canned green beans with some canned field peas and cook them the same way. Be sure to add a little oil or margarine.

MARDI GRAS RICE

For a colorful dish of rice that is pretty to serve your guests, cut up some red, green, and yellow bell peppers when they are all in season, and some red onions. Sauté them lightly in some margarine and stir into freshly cooked rice. Then lightly dust the top with some paprika.

CAJUN STUFFED POTATOES

6 baking potatoes
1/4 stick butter
1/2 pint cream
2 green onions with tops
1/2 cup grated cheddar cheese
1/4 cup chopped parsley
Salt and cayenne pepper to taste

Wash potatoes, oil skins, and bake 40 minutes in a hot oven (450°), or in a microwave according to directions. Remove from oven, cut in half, and scoop the cooked potato out of the shells. Add butter and cream and whip. Mix in onions, cheese and parsley and stuff shells. Sprinkle with paprika and bake 10 minutes in 400° oven.

(Author's Recipes)

Shady Bayou with Magnolia Trees and Pine Trees.

Are you a Purist?

Choose between a Crawfish Etouffée and a Crawfish Ragoût

Crawfish Etouffée has traveled outside of Cajun Country to New Orleans and to English North Louisiana, and now, all around the United States. It often has lost something in translation. The pure Cajun version of Crawfish Etouffée uses only the natural juices and fats of the crawfish and the juices of the vegetables used to season it. When a thick roux is made it becomes a stew, or Crawfish Ragoût (or Ragoût d'Ecrivisses). Some people like to dust in just a wee bit of flour, which does not change the color, but gives it a little thickening. However, since it is almost always served over rice, it really doesn't need any thickening.

Crawfish Etouffée

ECRIVISSES ETOUFFÉE
(Crawfish Etouffée or Smothered Crawfish)

1 lb. cleaned crawfish tails
   (Include crawfish fat)
1 stick margarine
1 onion, chopped fine
2 chopped green onions
1 rib celery, chopped
4 thin slices of lemon

1 tablespoon parsley
2 tablespoons chopped
   pimento (or red or green
   bell pepper)
1 teaspoon flour
Salt and cayenne pepper

Sauté onions and celery in margarine until soft. Add everything (including the fat which adds much of the flavor) except the crawfish tails and simmer for 10 minutes, sprinkling the flour over the contents of the pan. This is to give the sauce a little body, and you can add more if you like, but do not make a roux if you want your dish to be an authentic etouffée. Save the roux for crawfish stew, another recipe entirely. Now add the crawfish tails and simmer for 15 minutes. I sometimes like a light tomato taste in this dish and I add a small can of V-8 juice. Then it becomes "Crawfish Etouffée a la Tomate".

RAGOÛT D'ÉCRIVISSEE
(Crawfish Stew)

1 pound cleaned crawfish
   (Save crawfish fat)
3 tablespoons cooking oil
3 tablespoons flour
1 cup chopped onions
1/2 cup chopped green
   onions with tops
1/2 cup chopped bell pepper
1/2 cup chopped celery
1 clove garlic, minced

2 bay leaves
Pinch of ground cloves
1 teaspoon basil
1/2 teaspoon thyme
1 tablespoon lemon juice
1 tablespoon Worcestershire
   Sauce
6 sprigs parsley, chopped
Salt, cayenne, and Tabasco

Heat oil in a large frying pan, add flour when oil begins to bubble. Add the chopped vegetables and garlic at the same time. Reduce heat and stir continually until flour is a very dark brown. Add water (at least two cups) very gradually or grease will pop. Continue stirring and adding water until you have a creamy smooth gravy that is almost the color of dark chocolate, but not burned. This is a time consuming process that takes about one-half hour, but if you rush it you will have a lumpy mess. Now add the crawfish with the fat, add all of the herbs, plus the lemon juice and Worcestershire Sauce. Simmer for 20 minutes. Add salt, and cayenne pepper or Tabasco, or both and check for taste and seasonings before you add too much. It gets hotter as you eat more.

(Author's Recipes)

What Do You Have an "Envie" for Today?

An "envie", (pronounced ahn-vee, and closely related to the word envy) is a strong desire, a longing, or a craving for something; similar to the craving a pregnant mother may have for pickles and ice cream. There are many dishes on Grandmere's kitchen table that one could develop an envie for. Crawfish Etouffee; Oyster Soup, Tomato and Asparagus Salad Vinaigrette; Field Peas and Snaps; Mardi Gras Rice; Bread Pudding with Meringue; and mixed Kumquat and Watermelon Pickles. Here in the subtropics, there were orange trees, kumquats, loquats, figs, and pears. The peaches grew a little farther north.

OYSTER SOUP

1 quart oysters	2 sprigs parsley, chopped fine
Liquor from oysters	1 stalk celery, chopped fine
2 cups milk	1 tablespoon flour
1 cup cream	2 egg yolks
4 tablespoons butter	Salt and white pepper (or
2 green onions, chopped fine	cayenne if you prefer)

Scald milk but do not boil. Drain oysters. They may be used whole or cut in pieces. Melt butter and simmer oysters in it till edges curl. Remove and blend flour into butter, but do not brown. Gradually add milk to which beaten egg yolks have been added, much as you would make a cream sauce, but continue adding milk to make soup. Boil for just a minute. Add cream, vegetables, and seasoning. Heat thoroughly, but do not allow to boil again.

TOMATO AND ASPARAGUS SALAD VINAIGRETTE

Peel and slice tomatoes fairly thinly. Arrange on a platter. Lay stalks of cooked asparagus, (fresh, frozen, or canned) in an attractive pattern on top of the tomatoes. Pour the following vinaigrette dressing over the platter.

1/3 cup olive oil	2 tablespoons ketchup
1/3 cup tarragon vinegar	1 tablespoon chopped parsley
1/3 cup lemon juice	1 tablespoon basil
2 tablespoons sugar	1/4 cup sweet pickle relish
1/8 teaspoon dry mustard	1 chopped hard boiled egg
2 tablespoons chopped pimento	Salt and black pepper to taste

Mix vigorously and warm gently for a few minutes. Refrigerate overnight if possible before using. This also makes a good marinade. You may want to add the vinegar, lemon juice and sugar a little at a time to get the proper sweet and sour blend to suit your taste.

Bonne Année ... It's New Year's Day

The New Year was traditionally a time of merriment, celebration and fireworks for the Acadians. Christmas was kept as a true holy day, and in many French families, presents were not given out until New Year's Day. However, New Year's Day is also reserved as a holy day.

Note the Audubon Prints above the sideboard of the Indigo Bunting and the Painted Bunting (on the opposite page). The Acadian people used to trap these birds in little soft cages of wire and string, when it was still legal to do so, and keep them in their homes just as we keep canaries. Their song is a hushed, sweet warble, and the Cajuns called them the Bleu Évêque (the blue bishop) and the Pape Vert (little green bird). A "Pape" (pronounced pop) is any small bird, and the painted buntings are green their first year; then add their blue and red the second and third years.

CABBAGE ROLLS WITH TOMATO SAUCE

2 heads cabbage	1/4 teaspoon basil
1 pound ground pork or beef	1 cup cooked rice
1 cup chopped onions	2 eggs, beaten
1 clove garlic, minced	1/2 cup seasoned bread
1/4 cup chopped parsley	crumbs
1/4 teaspoon thyme	Salt and lemon pepper

Parboil large leaves of cabbage for a few minutes until pliable. Brown meat in a little oil. Add the onions and garlic halfway through and let them cook with the meat. Remove from pan, drain off excess oil and add a little water to make a light, natural gravy. Add some Worcestershire or steak sauce and some extra seasonings to this. Pour off and reserve. Put meat, rice, bread crumbs and all seasonings in pan. Mix thoroughly while heating through. Turn off heat, add eggs, and mix again. Place correct amount of stuffing in center of each cabbage leaf, fold in ends, roll up tightly and place in a large pot. If rolls are packed tight, they will hold their shape. Add the brown gravy which was reserved. This can be served as is, but some like cabbage rolls in a tomato sauce. Just add a can of tomato sauce or V-8 juice if you like. If you want to be fancy, serve with a dollop of sour cream on each cabbage roll.

STUFFED CABBAGE HEAD

Cut the whole center out of a medium size head of cabbage, leaving enough bottom and sides to hold the shape of the head. Chop the cabbage that has been removed. Fry one bulk package of Tennessee Sausage, breaking it apart well as you fry it. Before it gets completely browned, add one finely chopped onion, 2 tablespoons of ground parsley, 1 beaten egg, a pinch of thyme and enough cornbread crumbs to make a suitable mixture. Salt and lemon pepper to taste. Add milk slowly to make mixture hold together, but you will not need much. If there is some of the mixture left over, put it in a small baking dish and bake it at 350° for one-half hour.

Put a piece of cheesecloth around the head and place it in a colander over a large pot of boiling water. Turn heat down and steam, covered, until the entire head of cabbage is tender (at least an hour). Unwrap, after letting sit a little, being careful not to burn yourself in the steam. Serve in a large bowl, cutting away wedges of cabbage with the stuffing. Serve with vinegar and mustard to be used as your guests wish. This makes an attractive dish.

COLE SLAW WITH PINEAPPLE AND PECANS

Chop or shred cabbage finely, as you prefer. Add a little vinegar and sugar and mix thoroughly. Let stand overnight if possible, and then add mayonnaise and a little cream until you have a creamy mixture. Add drained crushed pineapple and either chopped pecans or chopped peanuts to give it a wonderful flavor, with salt and a little cayenne pepper. Serve immediately after adding the nuts.

The Overseer's House

No One Goes without Cabbage and Blackeyed Peas

Some superstition persists, but more for fun than anything. The belief still holds that eating cabbage on New Year's brings green "folding money" all year long, and serving blackeyed peas brings good luck. Consequently our sideboard boasts a variety of cabbage; Steamed Cabbage Wedges with Ham Slices; Cabbage Rolls with Tomato Sauce; A Cabbage Head Stuffed with Sausage Dressing; Cole Slaw with Pineapple and Pecans; and Sweet and Sour Red Cabbage. Accompaniments include Blackeyed Peas with Sautéed Mushrooms, Meat Pies, Sausage Bread, Corn Bread with Cracklin's, Rice Salad, Spiced Peaches, and Toasted Pecans, in addition to a Pineapple decoration for hospitality and some Champagne for the celebration.

MEAT PIES

1 pound ground pork	2 tablespoons Worcestershire
1 pound ground beef	Sauce
1 cup chopped green onions,	1 tablespoon lemon juice
tops and bottoms	Pinch of ground cloves
1 chopped bell pepper	Salt, black pepper and
1/4 cup chopped parsley	cayenne pepper to taste
	1/4 cup flour

Brown meat and add onions and other seasonings near end of browning. Cut off heat, add sauce and lemon juice, and stir in flour. If mixture seems too dry, some meat stock or a little water may be added.

CRUST

4 cups flour	2 teaspoons salt
1/2 cup melted shortening	2 eggs and 1 cup milk

Cut shortening into flour, add eggs and milk, and form into a ball. Chill. Roll thin and cut circles, using a saucer as a guide. Place 2 tablespoons of meat mixture on round of dough, fold over edges, press dampened edges together with a fork, and cook in deep fat until brown. These little pies can be brushed with melted butter or margarine and baked, but they are crispier if fried in deep fat until golden brown. They may be wrapped and stored in the freezer, and cooked at a later time.

SAUSAGE BREAD

Use your favorite all purpose bread recipe, or a packaged bread or roll mix, or buy the frozen bread that one thaws, lets rise, and then bakes. Roll it out into a reasonably thin rectangle and flour so that it can be handled easily. Fry some bulk Tennessee Sausage until almost brown, add some chopped onions, and finish browning. Spread this over the dough and sprinkle with shredded cheddar cheese. Fold about four inches of the bread in over the mixture. Then fold again, rather like making a jelly roll, but make it flat instead of round. When you have used up all of the dough and folded in the ends a bit to seal it, you should have a long, narrow, and flat loaf, not more than 5 inches wide. Bake according to the directions for your bread recipe. This can also be filled with crawfish instead of sausage.

(Author's Recipes)

... and Then Comes Lent.

Lent was always a solemn interlude in the yearly sequence of events in Acadian life. However, the limitation imposed by the insistence of the Church was hardly noticeable. Their immediate environment provided a continual and bountiful harvest of the fruits of the sea and their creativity in the kitchen knew no bounds. Long years of frugality had taught them to use everything at hand and to enhance its flavor with the seasonings provided by the land. Potato stew or egg stew, even without the addition of shrimp, can be indescribably delicious and remains a favorite even today when the church rules have been relaxed and Acadians are more affluent.

CRAWFISH PIES

1 lb. crawfish, ground coarsely, save fat	1 tablespoon butter
1/2 cup butter or oil	1 tablespoon flour
1/4 cup chopped bell pepper	1 cup half and half
1/4 cup chopped celery	3 chopped boiled eggs
1/3 cup chopped parsley	1 tablespoon Worcestershire Sauce
1/4 cup chopped green onions	Bread crumbs as needed
	Salt and pepper to taste

Sauté vegetables in a little olive oil, and then add the crawfish and continue simmering. Add crawfish fat and tomatoes, and simmer 20 minutes. Make a cream sauce in a separate pan, stirring the flour into the melted butter, and adding the cream slowly, stirring all the while. Add cream sauce to crawfish, stir in the chopped eggs, and heat a little longer. Season with salt and pepper and add a little of the bread crumbs if the mixture is too thin. Spoon into unbaked tart shells (or one large pie crust), and bake in 350° oven until browned, about 30 minutes. Makes about 16 tarts. Some cooks prefer a slightly sweet pie dough, but I think it takes away from the flavor of the crawfish.

CRAWFISH BISQUE

A huge amount of work is involved in making crawfish bisque, but the end result is worth every second of it.

50 pounds of crawfish	1/4 teaspoon ground cloves
10 onions	4 bay leaves
4 bell peppers	2 tablespoons thyme
1 bunch celery	3 tablespoons oregano
2 bunches green onions	5 raw eggs
2 bunches parsley	2 sticks butter, melted
10 pods garlic	10 cups bread crumbs
3 cans tomato paste	Salt and pepper to taste

Roux: Heat 1/2 cup oil until it begins to bubble, lower heat and carefully stir in 1/2 cup flour, continuing to stir until flour is dark brown. Add water slowly and carefully so that it does not make the grease pop, until you have the consistency of a good thick gravy. Add salt and pepper to taste.

You will want to buy crawfish that have already been boiled. Break off the tails and peel. Clean the "heads" (actually the shell which covers the thorax). Use a beer can opener upside down, pushing it away from you to shove everything out of this large red shell. When you are finished, rinse out the shells.

Grind all the vegetables and tail meat, mix thoroughly with all ingredients including tomato paste, eggs, butter and bread crumbs, but save the bay leaves to put in the gravy. Stuff the heads fully with this mixture and save in a pan. Reserve a little of the loose stuffing to put in the gravy. By now, you have probably run out of steam, so cover the stuffed heads and put them in the refrigerator overnight. You can start again in the morning.

Roll each head well in flour and fry them in a little hot oil until they start to brown. Meanwhile, heat the gravy well and add the leftover stuffing mixture to it. As the heads brown, drop them in the gravy and cook for at least an hour. Some cooks like to drop in slices of lemon. Serve over steaming hot rice.

(Author's Recipes)

Crawfish Bisque

Crawfish Pies

Although Lent is a Time of General Abstinance, Lenten Dishes Can Be Satisfying

Our table in front of the tiny cast-iron mantelpiece is set with some of the most typical Lenten dishes: Crawfish Bisque; Crawfish Pies; Corn and Crabmeat Soup; Turnip Greens; Potato Stew with Onions and Eggs; and Bell Pepper Halves, one stuffed with Shrimp Salad and the other with Crabmeat Salad. The dessert is Creole Cream Cheese and Strawberries. Crawfish Bisque is made by stuffing the "heads" (actually the body shell) with a crawfish meat mixture. It is so delicious that the big boys in the family like refills. They were often asked to place their empty shells around the bowl so that everyone could count them, and insure an equal share for all.

CREOLE CREAM CHEESE AND STRAWBERRIES

Clean strawberries and marinate overnight in Cointreau liqueur. Place a quantity of Creole Cream Cheese in each bowl. Add strawberries around the edges of the bowls, and sprinkle lightly with powdered sugar. Creole Cream Cheese is very much a Louisiana product. If you cannot buy it, I suppose the closest thing would be sour cream or yogurt. We also make a light summer dessert by freezing crushed pineapple and a little sugar with the Creole Cream Cheese.

Easter at the Overseer's House

Easter Sunday is "le Jour de Pâques", and when all the typically large families gather at Grandmere's house, it is quite a crowd. Often, the tables must be set in the yard to make room for everyone. Here we see the Ham which has been baked with an Apricot Glaze, and garnished with apricot halves and hardboiled eggs that have been peeled and tinted. Scalloped Potatoes and Peas with Pearl Onions go nicely with Ham, and we see a basket of Cajun Easter Eggs, some candy Easter Eggs, and a loaf of freshly baked bread.

ESCALLOPED POTATOES, A L'ACADIANE

Potatoes, boiled, cooled, peeled and sliced
3 tablespoons butter
3 tablespoons flour
1 cup heavy cream
1/2 cup grated cheddar cheese
1/4 cup chopped green onions
1/4 cup chopped bell peppers
Chopped parsley
Salt, pepper, and paprika

Melt butter, stir in flour and blend in heavy cream. Put a layer of sliced potatoes in the bottom of a baking dish. Sprinkle chopped vegetables over the top, saving some of each for other layers. Repeat this twice more. Add salt, white pepper, and grated cheese on top of each layer, as you go. Pour cream mixture over the top and sprinkle with a little paprika and parsley bits. Bake an hour and fifteen minutes at 350° until potatoes are done and lightly golden on top.

HAM WITH APRICOTS

Buy the nicest canned ham you can find with the least amount of fat. Slice it thickly and lay overlapping slices in a baking dish. Spread it with apricot jam which you have stirred well with a spoon so that you can spread it, and place apricot halves around the edge of the dish. Bake until it is hot and bubbly and slightly browning around the edges. Remove from oven.

Meanwhile, peel some hardboiled eggs and dye them in food coloring. They will not be as bright as regular dyed eggs, but will be in pretty pastel shades—a charming decoration for Easter.

MINTED PEAS WITH PEARL ONIONS

Cook fresh or frozen peas until tender and drain. Heat butter in a saucepan and add a little chopped fresh mint. Heat peas and cooked fresh or canned pearl onions in the minted butter until the whole mixture is well heated through. This makes a fresh tasting dish for Spring.

Cajun Easter Eggs are very Special

The Acadians, as always, have a way of making do with very simple things. Their tradition has always been to decorate hard boiled eggs by dying them with onion skins and printing them with clover leaves. They are charming, and very different from the brightly decorated eggs of many other peasant cultures. The color is a lovely warm tan, and the print of the clover remains in white. (See recipe below)

The "Lapin de Pâques" (Easter Bunny) brings Cajun Easter Eggs

CORN AND CRABMEAT SOUP

1 lb. lump crabmeat	1 cup chopped green onions
1/2 stick butter	with tender tops
1/4 cup flour	1 cup milk
4 ears corn (or use	1 cup half and half
canned cream corn)	Salt and white pepper

Cut the kernels off the cob and scrape for milk. White corn is nicest if you can get it. Melt butter in deep pan, add flour, and stir gently until blended. Do not let it darken. Add milk gradually, then add half and half, stirring gently and blending all the while. Add corn and green onions and cook a few minutes until they are tender. Add lump crabmeat and simmer till very hot and small bubbles form around the edge, but do not let boil. Serve immediately and garnish with sprinkles of chopped parsley.

TASTY POTATO STEW

3 tablespoons olive oil	1 bell pepper, cut in chunks
3 tablespoons flour	1 onion, cut in chunks
4 to 6 large potatoes	2 tablespoons steak sauce
6 hard boiled eggs	Parsley, thyme and basil
1/2 cup chopped shallots	to taste and pinch of cloves
2 stalks chopped celery	2 bay leaves, salt, and pepper

Brown flour in oil or margarine. Make a medium dark roux, and add water slowly, stirring until blended and thickened. Add potato which has been cut into chunky pieces, and all other vegetables and seasonings. Cook until done. This makes a very tasty meatless Lenten dish, but either shrimp or crawfish may be added to it to make it even better.

CAJUN EASTER EGGS

Acadian dyed eggs are traditionally decorated for Easter, but they would also be a decorative addition for a brunch. Save the dry brown outer skins of onions. I save them through the year in a mesh onion bag. Gently punch a tiny hole in large end of eggs with an egg piercer, large needle, or sharp point of a knife to prevent cracking. Pick some clover leaves, or any thin, small leaves such as climbing ferns, chickweed, or anything that will make an attractive pattern. Cut stockings in pieces large enough to cover eggs. Dampen the shells of the eggs thoroughly and press the leaves against the shell in some sort of pattern. Thick leaves will not work. Do one egg at a time. While holding leaves in place, stretch and wrap a piece of stocking around egg, twist tightly and tie securely with thread or string. Obviously you will have to remove your fingers as you carefully wrap the stocking across the leaves. Place eggs and plenty of onion skins in cold water, gradually bring to a boil, and heat just below boiling point for 30 minutes. Remove, cool, and cut away stockings. Remove leaves. Eggs will be a beautiful rosy brown with a pattern of white clover leaves or whatever leaves you have used. Some ferns and other leaves will leave a pretty pale green stain on the eggs.

(Author's Recipes)

The Gumbo Pot Can Create a Great Variety of Gumbos

Gumbo derives its name from the African word "gombo", which means okra, for the gelatinous okra was first used as a thickening agent for gumbo, which is a sort of thick soup. Visitors to Louisiana often confuse Gumbo and Jambalaya. Jambalaya is a rice dish, similar to the Spanish Paella, and may derive its name from "jambon", the French word for ham. Okra is not always put in Gumbo, for filé is often used as the thickening agent. It is a finely ground powder made from the leaves of the Sassafras tree, and it also adds an herb flavor to the dish. This is why you sometimes hear the term "Filé Gumbo". Gumbo is always made with a dark brown roux, and can be made thick or thin, but moderately thick is usually the approved consistency. It can be made with meat, poultry, or seafood, or any combination thereof. The gumbo is usually served with a large spoonful of Rice added at the last, a Creamy Potato Salad, and possibly a side dish of Broiled Tomatoes.

Chicken Gumbo

CHICKEN AND SAUSAGE GUMBO

1 large hen, cut up	1 clove garlic, crushed
1 lb. sausage, sliced	1 teaspoon thyme
4 tablespoons oil	1 teaspoon sage
4 tablespoons flour	Salt and pepper to taste
1 large onion, chopped	2 quarts water, or more
1 bell pepper, chopped	1/4 cup chopped parsley
2 stalks celery, chopped	1 tablespoon filé

Fry chicken pieces in oil and drain. Brown sausage (or andouille or ham) and drain. Save 4 tablespoons of the oil and brown the flour. Add water slowly over low heat so that it doesn't flame up. Add chicken, sausage, chopped vegetables and seasonings. Add parsley near end of cooking time. Simmer until chicken is tender. Add filé just as pot is removed from fire and stir in, or serve separately in a small bowl to be passed at the table and let each person serve himself. If added too early, it may become ropy as it is a thickener. Serve in large bowls with fluffy rice piled up in the center. Sprinkle chopped green onions or chives over the top.

SEAFOOD GUMBO

1/2 cup flour	1 lb. crabmeat
1/2 cup oil	1 quart oysters with liquor
1 large onion, chopped	2 bay leaves
1 clove garlic, minced	1 tablespoon Worcestershire
1/2 bell pepper, chopped	Sauce
1/4 cup parsley, chopped	2 quarts water
2 lb. shrimp or crawfish	Salt, pepper, Tabasco and filé to taste

Make a roux by browning flour in hot oil until dark brown. Add water slowly, gradually smoothing into a paste. Continue adding all the water. Add vegetables and cook 30 minutes. Add crabmeat with some claws and broken body chunks. Add bay leaves and all seasonings, but save parsley until near the end of the cooking time and the filé for the last. Cook 15 minutes. Add shrimp and oysters and cook until oysters curl (5 minutes). Cut heat, add filé and serve.

Filé powder is made from Sassafras leaves and is a thickener. Start with 1 tablespoon and add more if necessary, or put a bowl on the table for individual serving. Serve gumbo with rice.

(Author's Recipes)

Seafood Gumbo

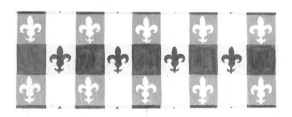

The Fleur de Lis (a stylized lily flower) is a symbol used by France, and so it was dear to the hearts of the French Acadians. It is also used as a symbol of the Trinity, so it also had a religious significance for them.

Shrimp & Okra gumbo

Manger a la Fortune du Pot...
A Covered Dish Potluck Church Supper

Potluck supper translates almost literally into French, "Eat of the luck of the pot". No one ever seems to plan what will be brought to a covered dish supper, but somehow, the menu is always well balanced. Here we have a motley group of pots and dishes, holding a diverse collection of recipes: Sausage Jambalaya; Chicken Fricassée; Pink Lemonade; Field Peas and Snaps; Green Bean, Beet and Onion Salad; Cole Slaw; Eggplant Casserole; Raspberry Shortbread; and small French Bread Loaves (called Frogs). Fricassée always sounds so much more exciting when the Cajuns say it: (Free-kah-say! sounds like an explosion).

COUNTRY COLE SLAW

1 small head cabbage	2 tablespoons mustard
1/2 cup vinegar	Milk or buttermilk as needed
1/2 cup sugar	Salt, pepper, and 1/2 cup
1 cup mayonnaise	finely chopped peanuts

Slice or chop one head of cabbage as finely as possible. Mix vinegar and sugar and pour over cabbage. Mix well and let stand for at least two hours, or preferably overnight in the refrigerator. Mix mustard into mayonnaise and add to mixture. Stir thoroughly and then moisten with milk or buttermilk until creamy. Add seasonings and chopped peanuts just before serving and mix thoroughly.

RASPBERRY SQUARES

1 box butter cake mix	1 egg
1/2 cup chopped pecans	1 jar diet or unsugared
1/4 cup margarine	raspberry jam

Grease an oblong baking dish and dust lightly with flour. Stir cake mix in a large bowl, knocking out all of the lumps. Add pecans, margarine and beaten egg and mix thoroughly by hand. It will stick to beaters and become hard to handle. Dump into baking dish and spread around. Push into corners and smooth out with fingers if necessary. Whip jam with spoon until it spreads easily and cover the cake mixture with it. Bake at 325° for 30 minutes, until bubbly and slightly brown. Cool and cut into squares.

SAUSAGE JAMBALAYA

1/2 pound Chaurice (hot sausage)
1/2 pound Andouille
1/4 pound Tasso (optional)
1 large onion, chopped
1 bell pepper, chopped
4 stalks celery, chopped
5 cloves minced garlic
1 1-pound can tomatoes
2 cups rice
3 cups chicken stock
2 cups smoked ham, diced
4 green onions, sliced
1/4 cup parsley, chopped
Salt and pepper to taste
Tabasco to taste

Sauté hot sausage and Tasso in oil if necessary, for several minutes. In same oil add onions, cook until tender, then add bell pepper and celery. Cook until browned.

Add rice and stir until coated in the oil. Add tomatoes, chicken stock, garlic, sliced andouille, and ham. Bring mixture to a boil. Cover and let simmer about 30 minutes or until rice is done. Before serving, add green onions and parsley. Serve hot with French bread and a green salad.

Recipe from Cookin' Cajun Cooking School in New Orleans

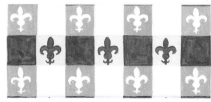

Wooden Country Church

The Acadians are a Faithful People

Almost the entire Acadian population embraces the Catholic faith. Getting to church was very difficult sometimes. Often they had to come by boat, but usually by walking long distances, or on horseback or by horse and buggy. Sometimes, when the shrimp fleet was out in the Gulf and the shrimp were running well, they could not afford to leave their good fortune and come into church, because that was their livelihood, and shrimp did not always bring such high prices as at present. However, they always wore a cross around their neck, and said their prayers, and often said that the "little tin Jesus" (around their neck) then allowed them to stay out and finish the job.

GREEN BEAN, BEET AND ONION SALAD

1 package frozen green beans
1 can beets, sliced thin
1 onion, sliced thin
1/4 cup olive oil
1/4 cup tarragon vinegar
Salt and pepper to taste
1 tablespoon chopped bell pepper
1 tablespoon chopped parsley
1 tablespoon chopped chives
1/2 teaspoon paprika

Cook beans, drain, and mix with beets and onions, which have been pulled apart into rings. Mix all other ingredients and beat well. Add a little sugar if desired. Pour over salad and chill thoroughly.

CHICKEN FRICASSEE

One 4 pound hen
2 large onions, minced
6 tablespoons flour
6 tablespoons cooking oil
4 cups hot water
1/4 cup green onion tops
1/8 cup parsley, chopped
Salt and pepper to taste

Cut up chicken as for frying, season and cook until brown in hot cooking oil. Remove from oil and add flour, browning slowly until dark golden brown. Add onions and cook until soft. Add chicken to this and also the water, and cook until chicken is tender. Keep gravy the consistency of thick cream. Toward end of cooking time, add chopped green onion tops and parsley. Serve with potatoes or rice.

SPICY EGGPLANT CASSEROLE

4 medium size eggplants
1 tomato, chopped
1 large onion, chopped
1 bell pepper, chopped
4 tablespoons oil
1 pound ground meat
1 can tomato paste
1/2 teaspoon basil
Seasoned bread crumbs
Salt and cayenne to taste

Peel (or not, if you prefer) eggplants and cut into large cubes, boil until tender. Drain extremely well, preferably overnight. Meanwhile, sauté tomato, onion, and pepper in hot oil. Cook ground meat separately and drain off extra oil. Add tomato paste to meat in pan and cook on low heat until paste begins to darken and thicken. Add all vegetables and basil to meat mixture, and drained eggplant cubes. Mix thoroughly, add salt and pepper to taste, and add bread crumbs until mixture is not mushy, but has some texture. Spoon into large baking dish, sprinkle with Parmesan cheese and paprika, and bake until well done and browned. (Add minced garlic to recipe if you like.) We do cook things to death in South Louisiana, but it surely does taste good!

(Author's Recipes)

35

Joyeux Noel! ... A Simple Cajun Christmas Dinner

Christmas in the bayou country didn't necessarily mean turkey. With good hunting in the winter, the main dish might be any sort of delicous game. Smoked ham from an earlier boucherie might grace the holiday table or a beautiful baked fish. Turkeys did not thrive in the wet marshes and large grocery stores were not plentiful. A beautifully glazed roast duck was appropriate, with side dishes of rice dressing and colorful maque choux, which was apparently learned from the Indians. Often, if the head of the household was far from home in the winter, trapping and camping in the marshes, he could not afford the time to come in for Christmas. In that event, Christmas was merely held over till his arrival home, and then his price for the pelts could buy presents for all.

Maque Choux

ROAST DUCK

3 oranges	1 cup dry vermouth
6 pound duck	2 tablespoons sugar
1/4 cup butter	1 1/2 tablespoons vinegar
1 cup chicken stock	3 tablespoons curacao
1 lemon	2 teaspoons cornstarch

Dress and clean duck. Rub with salt and pepper and brown well in melted butter in a heavy pan. Roast at 400° for 20 minutes, then at 350° for about an hour in a covered baking dish. Baste frequently with dry vermouth.

Melt the sugar in a small pan, add vinegar, and caramelize. Remove duck from oven, drain off fat, and add chicken stock to the same pan. Now add the juice of the 3 oranges, a little grated orange rind (the zest, not the inner white part), the juice of a lemon and the curacao. Blend in the cornstarch and the caramelized sugar. Cook for about 10 minutes. Return duck to pan, spoon sauce over duck slowly, heat a little more, while continuing to baste with sauce until duck is glazed. Garnish with orange slices and curly parsley.

ROAST HEN

Rub hen inside and out with butter or oleo and salt and pepper. Make a mixture of one apple, cut into cubes, 1/2 onion cut in chunks, mandarin orange sections, and some green grapes. Add some toasted croutons and enough port wine to moisten the mixture. Stuff the hen with this mixture. Roast on a rack in 375° oven, basting continually with butter or oleo. The hen may also be stuffed with rice and oyster dressing. See recipe.

CAJUN/INJUN MAQUE CHOUX WITH TOMATOES

1 cup white lye hominy	1/4 cup diced bell pepper
1 cup yellow corn	1/4 cup pimento bits
1 cup white shoepeg corn	Dash of lemon juice or vinegar
2 cups stewed tomatoes	Salt, pepper, and hot sauce
1/4 cup chopped shallots	to taste

Canned or frozen vegetables may be used, but fresh ones are better. Cut corn from cob, and catch all scrapings and milk. Sauté hominy kernels and yellow and white corn in a little bacon fat or butter. Some crumbled bacon may be added to the recipe if you wish. Add chopped vegetables to corn while sautéing. Stew tomatoes until soft and well broken up. Add lemon juice and seasonings to tomatoes while stewing. Add tomatoes to corn mixture and bring to a rolling boil. Reduce heat and simmer long enough for the corn to get tender. This makes a very colorful dish. The Acadians learned it from the Indians.

MANDARIN PINEAPPLE SWEET POTATOES

Bake six to eight sweet potatoes at about 350° until tender. When cool, peel and slice or cut in chunks. Drain one can mandarin orange sections and one large can chunk pineapple (or crushed pineapple, if you prefer). Mix potatoes and fruit and arrange in a baking dish. Cover with brown sugar and pats of butter and return to the oven until bubbly and syrupy.

BUTTERY BRUSSELS SPROUTS

Steam cleaned Brussels sprouts until very tender, 20 to 30 minutes. Salt and pepper, preferable with white pepper. Melt 1/2 stick of butter and drizzle over the top when they are served. Roll them around a little to be sure they are well coated with the butter.

A Réveillon for Father Christmas

A Réveillon was a midnight supper that was held after Midnight Mass on Christmas Eve. It was a time for hushed merriment, because the little ones had already been put to bed. If Papa Noel comes down the chimney, he will see a platter of Roast Duck and Roast Chicken, Creamed Mushrooms in a Nest of Wild Rice, Maque Choux, Baked Sweet Potatoes with Pineapple and Mandarin Orange Sections, Ambrosia, Buttery Brussels Sprouts, and Preserved Kumquats with chunks of Pickles Watermelon.

CREAMED MUSHROOMS
IN A WILD RICE NEST

Cook wild rice according to directions or use a wild rice mix. If you are not using a mix, season the drained rice well. Heat a can of small whole mushrooms, jarred or fresh, in a light onion soup, (a can or a mix). If you are using the can, do not add any water. Lift the mushrooms out of the soup and mix the soup with the rice. Mound the hot mixture of rice in a serving bowl, hollow out a nest in the center and place the mushrooms in the nest.

Sunday Dinner ...

The church was the focal point of the village, and the priest was a part of their everyday life. He was Father to everyone, and present at all of the social functions. There was a closeness and a fellowship in the community that is hard to find today in larger towns. He would almost surely be invited to someone's home for dinner every Sunday. This particular church is located in Acadian Village, a tourist attraction in Lafayette.

Old White Brick Church at Acadian Village

SPICY CAJUN BROWN GRAVY

Make a roux as follows: Use equal amounts of flour and shortening. Add the flour to the hot shortening, lower heat slightly and brown flour while constantly stirring and smoothing. Work at this very slowly because you will surely spoil it if you rush it. A good roux may take a half an hour to make. You must constantly scrape the bottom and pull up the darkening flour so that it won't burn and blacken. As you gradually blend it in, the roux will begin to turn to a nice rich brown. It should get to be the color of melted chocolate and look as creamy, if you like it dark, but be sure to remove it from the fire before it burns the least bit or it will taste badly. Now add some cold water, put it back on a low heat, and keep adding water slowly. You can add chopped onion, pepper, etc. at any point, even to the shortening, but it interferes somewhat with the blending, so add it with the water. Stir in water until you achieve the desired consistency and let it cook a long while, or you will have the raw taste of flour that has not cooked.

ACADIAN STUFFED ROAST

4 to 6 pound roast	1 onion
1 red bell pepper	2 stalks celery
1 green bell pepper	Olive oil
3-4 cloves garlic	Salt, red pepper, and black pepper

Rub the roast with olive oil. Cut all of the vegetables into chunks, and the garlic into smaller pieces. Make deep cuts in the roast and stuff with as much of the vegetables as you can squeeze in. Add the remainder to the gravy. Place the roast in a hot oven, 450°, for fifteen minutes to sear the juices in, and then reduce to 350°. Roast 20 minutes per pound for rare meat, 25 minutes for medium, and 30 minutes for well done. Serve with pan gravy or Spicey Cajun Brown Gravy. See Recipe.

COUNTRY CORN MAQUE CHOUX

1 red bell pepper, diced	1/8 cup olive oil
1 green bell pepper, diced	1/2 teaspoon savory
2 stalks celery, sliced	1/2 teaspoon basil
1 onion, diced	Salt and cayenne pepper
2 cans corn niblets	to taste
1/4 cup oleo	

Heat oleo and olive oil together. Add diced vegetables and cook until just tender but not too soft. Add corn niblets (canned or fresh) and seasonings, and toss lightly with vegetables, continuing to heat until everything is hot. Cubed chicken or ham may be added to this for a one dish meal.

GREEN BEANS AND SAUSAGE ZYDECO

2 links smoked sausage, sliced thin	1 red bell pepper, diced
2 cans green beans, cut or French style	2 stalks celery, sliced
	1/2 teaspoon tarragon
	Salt and cayenne pepper

The sausage may be fresh, smoked, or andouille sausage, according to your choice. Fry the sausage and drain off most of the fat. Toss the bell pepper and celery lightly in the remaining fat until barely tender, and add the seasoning and the beans, (which may be fresh). Continue cooking until mixture is well heated.

"Zydeco" is the black version of cajun music and is accompanied by rubbing on a metal sort of washboard (a "frattoir"). The musicians often sang a favorite song about putting "too much salt in the beans". The French word for "the beans" is "les haricots". Run together it sounds like lesaricot with a roll on the "r" which makes it sound like a "d". Thus "les haricots" has become "zydeco", the nickname for the type of music.

38

... and Cook Enough for All the Relatives

There is no telling who will drop in for dinner; possibly Tantes et Oncles (aunts and uncles) and the Cousines et Cousins (pronounced Couzeens and Couzans, i.e. Girl cousins and boy cousins), and Pere Boudreaux, the Priest. Maman has prepared a Stuffed Roast, with garlic and red and green bell pepper bits stuffed into small cuts in the meat, and she will serve it with Spicy Cajun Brown Gravy, Corn Maque Choux, Green Beans Zydeco with Sausage, and Parslied Rice. The food for this shot was prepared at Chez Pastor's in Lafayette, thanks to Pat Pastor and Maugie, who is the best "Maman" anywhere.

A Typical White Acadian Cottage at Acadian Village in Lafayette

SALADE MARINÉE

Tear lettuce into pieces, chop some fresh parsley finely, cut tomatoes into chunks and chop celery and cucumber into fine dice. Save a few thin slices of cucumbers to decorate the plates, and a few sprigs of parsley. Cover salad plates with lettuce, place chunks of tomatoes around, and make a mound of chopped vegetables in center.

Dressing:

4 tablespoons olive oil	1/2 teaspoon mustard
4 tablespoons cane vinegar	1 teaspoon paprika
1/2 tablespoon sugar	2 tablespoons sweet relish
1 tablespoon lemon juice	Salt and cayenne pepper

Shake until thoroughly mixed and pour over salad.

POTATO FARCI EN RAMEQUIN
(Stuffed Potato in a ramekin)

Bake as many potatoes as needed, peel and mash. Whip with butter and heavy cream, salt and white pepper. Do not let mixture get too thin. Place in large individual ramekins and cover with shredded cheese and a dot of butter. Heat in oven until bubbly.

FRENCH TOAST ROUNDS

Slice a small loaf of French bread very thin. Spread with butter and sprinkle with garlic powder. Toast slowly in 325° oven until very dry, light brown, and crispy. Serve with soup or salad. These rounds can be served perfectly plain without anything on them.

Filet with Marchand de Vin Sauce

Company Comes to Dinner on the Bayou

A steak was pretty high living in the old days, because not much beef was raised on the bayou. The mosquitoes gave them quite a problem. However, the Cajuns over around Crowley raised cattle in the flat marshlands known as the "wet prairies". It was something like the Old West, because they had brands, cattle thieves, and even vigilantes in those days. This beautiful thick Filet is served with a rich Marchand de Vin Sauce. The name translates as a sauce fit for a wine merchant. The steak is accompanied by a Broiled Tomato, Potato Farci (Stuffed Potato) in a ramequin (ramekin), a Salade Marinée and Rounds of toasty brown French Bread. Again, the food was planned by Maugie Pastor, who says little Cajun children are made of gumbo, boudin, and sauce piquante.

RICE AND OYSTER DRESSING

3 cups cooked rice
2 cups chopped cooked
   giblets
1 pint oysters and their liquid
Small bunch of green onions,
   chop tops and bottoms

1 stalk celery, chopped
2 small green peppers, cut fine
1/2 cup minced parsley
1/2 cup minced parsley
Thyme and sage as desired
Giblet liquid as needed
Salt and pepper to taste

Sauté green onions, celery, parsley and peppers in butter on low heat until soft and yellowed. Stir rice mixture with other seasonings. Oysters may be added whole or cut in pieces. Add giblets and liquid from oysters and giblets as needed. Stuff fowl with mixture and bake any remainder in a covered dish at 325° for about 40 minutes.

As you can see, dirty rice and rice dressing are very similar in character. Actually dirty rice can be used as a dressing and rice dressing can be served in a separate serving dish from the bird, so there is great overlap.

(from Nancy Jensen)

BEEF FILET MARCHAND DE VIN

4 filets of beef, trimmed,
   cut 2 to 4 inches thick
Light oil

Black and red pepper
Salt
Marchand de Vin Sauce

Let meat come to room temperature and preheat broiler. Rub all of the outside of the filet with a light oil. Rub black or red pepper or both, and salt over the outside of the steak. Have rack 4 inches below the broiler if filet is thick, and higher if it is thinner. Place the steaks in a pan, or place a pan underneath to catch the drippings. Broil for about 4 minutes on each side if you prefer a rare steak. Using a paper towel for protection, you can press your finger on the surface of the steak. If it is soft it will still be rare. It becomes hard when it is well done. A medium steak will be halfway between. Serve with a rich Marchand de Vin Sauce. (See below)

MARCHAND DE VIN SAUCE
(Wine Merchant Sauce)

First make a rich brown sauce (which you can make ahead) in a separate pan. Sauté a finely chopped onion in 2 tablespoons of butter. Add some freshly ground black pepper, a little salt, and 2 tablespoons of flour. Brown the flour and slowly add one can of beef stock, a little crushed garlic, and fresh or canned sliced mushrooms. Continue heating and stirring until the whole amount is reduced by at least half. This should be very concentrated. (You can buy rich brown sauce in a jar. It is sometimes known as Demi-Glace Sauce.)

Make a brown gravy with two tablespoons of oil and two tablespoons of flour, stirring until dark brown and adding a little water and 1/2 cup or more of red wine. Add these last ingredients gradually, stirring until smooth, and adding more water or wine if needed. Then add the rich brown sauce from the other pan and cook until fairly thick. Add the drippings from the pan and finish heating the sauce.

(Author's Recipes)

Cottage on the Bayou

Courir de Mardi Gras in Mamou.

Cajuns Go to Mardi Gras and "Laissez Les Bons Temps Rouler"!

Laissez Les Bons Temps Rouler means let the good times roll, and the Cajuns really know how to do that. In the country around Mamou, they have their own "Courir de Mardi Gras" or "running of the Mardi Gras". A small band of men in costumes and masks, mount horses and ride around to neighboring farms. They are led by a Capitaine who never wears a mask. They proceed to "make the macaque" (make monkey shines) and are given chickens, onions, etc. to make a gumbo. The Capitaine tries to keep some semblance of order as they stand up on the horses backs and dance.

Now, of course, they have to go to Mardi Gras in New Orleans sometimes, and some stayed on and taught the city folk how to cook Cajun. The Cookin' Cajun Cooking School in New Orleans prepared a tasty meal for us: Pork Chops Stuffed with Breadcrumbs, Spinach and Pecans; French Onion Soup with a Slice of French Bread Toast and Melted Cheese; Parslied Butter Beans with Shallots; Baked Tomatoes with Hot Pepper Jelly and Baked Apples with Brown Sugar, Butter, Raisins and Chopped Pecans. What a setting, on the Mississippi, with the Cajun Queen passing in the background.

BAKED TOMATOES WITH HOT PEPPER JELLY

2 large firm tomatoes (preferably Creole types)
Pepper Jelly (Creole Delicacies Brand)
Chopped parsley and seasoned bread crumbs

Preheat broiler. Wash tomatoes and cut in halves. Place halves in baking dish. Cover each half with two teaspoons pepper jelly. Sprinkle bread crumbs on top. Broil 10 minutes, approximately. Garnish with parsley.

BAKED APPLES WITH RAISINS, PECANS AND BROWN SUGAR

4 large Rome apples, washed and cored
2 tablespoons butter
1/2 cup chopped pecans
3/4 cup packed brown sugar
1/2 cup raisins
1 cup orange juice (optional)

Melt butter and brown sugar in saucepan. Add pecans and raisins, making a syrup. Arrange apples in a baking dish with 1 cup water (or 1 cup orange juice). Fill apples with pecan-raisin mixture. Cover tightly with foil and bake in a preheated 350° oven for about 20 to 25 minutes (or microwave with plastic wrap for 15 minutes).

All Recipes on this page are from the Cookin' Cajun Cooking School in New Orleans

PORK CHOPS WITH SPINACH AND PECAN STUFFING

4 thick cut pork chops with pocket for stuffing
1 (10 oz.) pkg. frozen chopped spinach, cooked and squeezed dry
1 cup Italian bread crumbs
2 tablespoons melted butter
1/2 cup chopped toasted pecans
Oil

Heat oil in a large skillet (preferably cast iron). Make stuffing by mixing together the spinach, bread crumbs, pecans and butter. Stuff pork chop pockets full. Add to hot oil and brown well on both sides. Lower heat, cover and cook about 30 minutes.

FRENCH ONION SOUP

1 quart beef stock or 2 cans beef broth (double strength) and 2 cans water
4 teaspoons Worcestershire Sauce
1 stick butter
2 cups thinly sliced onions
4 to 6 French Bread slices
4 to 6 Swiss cheese slices
Butter for bread

Melt butter in saucepan. Add onions and sauté about 5 minutes, stirring often. Add beef stock and Worcestershire Sauce. Simmer 20 minutes. Lightly butter bread slices and toast them. Place slice of toasted bread in bottom of each soup bowl. Ladle soup into bowls. Top with slice of Swiss cheese. Run under broiler flame to melt cheese. (Or run in microwave until cheese melts.)

BUTTER BEANS WITH SHALLOTS

Slice six shallots (green onions) thinly, including the tender green tops. Cook two 10 oz. boxes frozen butter beans (or fresh) in a small amount of water with 1/2 stick of butter in a saucepan and salt, and black or white pepper to taste. Add chopped shallots and cook another two or three minutes.

Cajun Cookin' Comes out of the Bayou Land ...

Now that Cajun Cooking has become so popular, the visitors to that city are trying to learn how to do it, and the Cookin' Cajun Cooking School is happy to provide a classroom for them. They are going to teach us how to cook Cajun Chicken and Spaghetti and we will discover that it is a wee bit different from Italian Spaghetti. It will be somewhat lighter, with more spices and more vegetables, and hot with cayenne (red) pepper.

CAJUN CHICKEN AND SPAGHETTI

1 fryer, cut up, or 8 of your favorite pieces of chicken	1 (16 oz.) can stewed tomatoes
1 lb. spaghetti, cooked and drained	2 bay leaves
1 onion, chopped	1/4 teaspoon thyme
1/2 bell pepper, chopped	Oil
2 cloves garlic, chopped	Seasoning for chicken, 1 teaspoon each cayenne (red) pepper, white pepper, black pepper, and salt
2 (16 oz.) cans tomatoes	

Season chicken with seasoning mix and brown in oil. Remove and drain on paper towels. In Dutch oven (or heavy pot) use 3 tablespoons oil from browning chicken and sauté onion 2 minutes. Add bell pepper and sauté 3 minutes. Add tomatoes and stewed tomatoes, garlic, bay leaves and thyme. Add chicken pieces, cover and simmer about 1 hour and 15 minutes. Remove bay leaves. Pour over cooked pasta on warm platter.

EGG, OLIVE and ANCHOVY SALAD WITH CAPERS and MUSTARD DRESSING

6 peeled, hard boiled eggs	1 small jar pimento stuffed olives, drained and sliced
Romaine lettuce, 6 to 8 leaves, washed and dried	Pinch salt and white pepper
1 can anchovies	

Tear lettuce into bite size pieces and arrange on plate. Cut eggs into quarters and put all over lettuce. Place anchovies all over salad. Place olive slices over the top.

Dressing:

1/2 cup mayonnaise	3 teaspoons Creole mustard
8 olives, sliced	

Mix well and drizzle all over salad.

Cajun Chicken and Spaghetti

ROCKEFELLER SAUCE

4 tablespoons butter	1 tablespoon anchovy paste
2 stalks chopped celery	1 tablespoon ketchup
6 chopped green onions	1/4 cup Herbsaint or Pernod
1 bunch chopped parsley	1 stick softened butter
1 10-oz. pkg. frozen spinach (cooked and drained)	Salt and pepper to taste
	Tabasco to taste

Melt 4 tablespoons butter, sauté celery, green onions, and parsley until tender. Add spinach. Place ingredients in food processor, and purée. Add anchovy paste, ketchup, and Herbsaint. Season to taste. Add remainder of stick of butter. Season.

(The "Country Cajuns" have borrowed this recipe from the Creole plantation owners.)

CREAMY PECAN PRALINES

1 cup brown sugar	1 cup white sugar
1/2 cup evaporated milk	2 tablespoons butter
1/4 teaspoon vanilla	1 cup pecans

Combine sugars and milk. Bring to a boil, stirring occasionally. Add butter, pecans, and vanilla. Mix completely and then do not stir anymore. Cook until temperature reaches 236° (softball stage). Cool about 5 minutes. Beat until thickened. Pour out onto a well-greased surface and allow to harden.

All Recipes on this page are from the Cookin' Cajun Cooking School in New Orleans

... and Turns up in the Big City!

In addition to the Cajun Chicken and Spaghetti, they have concocted a wonderfully rich Mardi Gras Bean Soup made from a colorful variety of dried beans; some Garlic Toast; a plate of Artichokes with Cajun Spinach Sauce, and a tasty Egg, Olive and Anchovy Salad with Capers and Mustard Dressing. The Cajuns are very fond of Anchovies. Dessert will be Creamy Rum Pralines and Chocolate Pralines.

ARTICHOKES WITH CAJUN SPINACH SAUCE

Plunge the artichoke hearts into a large pot of boiling water and boil gently for 30 or more minutes. Pull outer leaf to see if it comes off gently, to discover when they are done. Stick a fork into the bottom to see if it is tender. Turn upside down to drain. The stem, too, is edible if you cut it off and pull off the heavy outer fibers. Serve very hot with a bowl of Cajun Spinach Sauce.

Wash one pound of spinach well and remove tough stems. Cook in a large pot of boiling water for 5 minutes, or longer, if large leaves. Drain thoroughly in a colander, (or use frozen spinach). Chop well. Braise in 2 tablespoons butter in a large sauté pan. Add a cup of chicken stock and a cup of heavy cream. Stir in 1 teaspoon of dry mustard, 1/2 teaspoon of nutmeg, and salt and cayenne pepper to taste. A little Parmesan cheese may be added to this if desired. Cook down until thick enough to be a dipping sauce for the artichoke leaves. If you want the sauce to be really piquante, add a dash or two of Tabasco.

REMOULADE SAUCE

1 medium onion	2 teaspoons salt
1 bunch green onions	1/2 cup Creole mustard
1 stalk celery	2 tablespoons lemon juice
2 cloves garlic	2 tablespoons vinegar
1/4 cup parsley	1 tablespoon Worcestershire
1 tablespoon paprika	sauce
1/4 teaspoon cayenne pepper	4 shakes Tabasco
	3/4 cup oil (vegetable)

Combine all ingredients except oil in food processor. Turn on and slowly dribble in the oil. Allow flavors to marry for 24 hours or at least 20 minutes. Season to taste.

(This is a recipe that the Country Cajuns took home from the big city of New Orleans, but "c'est bon, yes"!)

Recipes on this page are from
Cookin' Cajun Cooking School in New Orleans

The Cookin' Cajun Cooking School, located in the Riverwalk Market Place, offers classes on a daily basis, 11 AM to 1 PM.

N'Orleans learns to season with Tasso

Tasso is a dried meat which is similar to jerky, but very hot. It can be used for cooking with many things, both as an addition to content of the dish, and for seasoning vegetables and soups. The Cookin' Cajun Cooking School has used it with oysters in a cream sauce to pour over Fettucine. Served alongside the Oysters with Tasso, Cream and Fettucine are; Okra and Tomatoes; Beet Salad with Onion Rings and Green Onions Sticks; Banana Muffins; and Sugared Pecans.

OYSTERS WITH TASSO, CREAM, AND FETTUCINE

3 dozen oysters	12 oz. pasta, cooked and
1/4 cup tasso, minced	drained
1 stick butter	6 shallots (green onions),
1 pint half and half	chopped
	Italian cheese, grated

Poach oysters lightly in their own liquid for about 3 minutes. Strain, saving broth. Drain oysters on paper towels and check for pieces of shell. Melt butter in sauté pan. Add tasso and cook 2 to 3 minutes. Add chopped shallots and cook 2 minutes. Add half and half cream and oyster broth and bring to a boil. Lower heat and simmer about 5 minutes. Add poached oysters and simmer another 3 minutes. Pour over pasta and sprinkle with Italian cheese.

(Author's note: This dish gets its seasoning from the hot tasso. If you cannot find tasso, substitute small pieces of ham or bacon or smoked turkey, but add extra seasoning.)

SUGARED PECANS

1/2 pound pecans	1/2 teaspoon cinnamon
1 cup sugar	1 cup water (or 1 cup
1 teaspoon vanilla	orange juice)

Cook sugar and water (or juice) 5 minutes in heavy cast iron or aluminum frying pan. Stir continually until syrup begins to cook down. Syrup will begin to look slightly crystallized. Add vanilla, cinnamon (and orange zest if you wish). Set pan in a place to cool for a short while. Place back on stove, and simmer slowly, preferably with a protective mat between the pan and the heat, and stir fairly vigorously and constantly until sugar starts to melt. Pour on marble surface or buttered cookie sheet placed over a cooling rack. Separate as they are drying.

(Sugared pecan halves in various flavors may be obtained from Creole Delicacies and other confectionaries in New Orleans.)

Recipes on this page are from the Cookin' Cajun Cooking School in New Orleans

Cajun Cookin' Becomes Gourmet, ... for the Uninitiated

Although Cajun Cooking to the Acadians may be everyday cooking, it is usually such an unusual and exciting taste for the visitor who has not savored it before, that it becomes a new and exotic experience for gourmet and gourmand alike.

OKRA AND TOMATOES

1 lb. fresh or frozen okra, sliced	1 clove garlic, minced
1 (16 oz.) can stewed tomatoes	1/4 cup oil
1 onion, chopped	1 tablespoon vinegar
	Salt, pepper, and cayenne

Heat oil. Add okra and vinegar and cook until all ropiness is gone and seeds turn pink. Add onion and sauté another 2 minutes. Add tomatoes, garlic, salt and peppers. Bring to a boil. Lower heat and simmer 15 to 20 minutes.

(Optional: A small can of corn may be added in last 5 minutes.)

*Recipe from Cookin' Cajun
Cooking School in New Orleans*

SHRIMP AND OKRA GUMBO

2 tablespoons oil	1/2 teaspoon crushed thyme
1 tablespoon vinegar	1/2 teaspoon cayenne pepper
2 lbs. fresh okra (can use frozen)	1 tablespoon Worcestershire sauce
4 tablespoon oil	1 teaspoon liquid crab boil (optional)
4 tablespoon flour	2 qts. seafood or chicken stock (or water)
1 large onion, chopped	2 lbs. shrimp
1 bell pepper, chopped	1 pint oysters and oyster water (optional)
2 stalks celery, chopped	1/2 cup parsley and green onions, chopped
1/2 cup lean ham, diced (optional)	
1 pod garlic, minced	
1 16-oz. can tomatoes, cut up	
2 bay leaves	

Wash and dry okra, remove stems, slice in 1/4 inch rounds. Heat 2 tablespoons oil in heavy saucepan (do not use black iron). Saute¹ okra and vinegar in oil until all ropiness is gone, stirring often. In another pot, make a good, dark roux with oil and flour. Add onion, celery and bell pepper. Saute¹ unti limp. Add diced ham and garlic. Add tomatoes. Cook 10 minutes, stirring often. Add okra. Add stock and seasonings. Cook 30 minutes.

Peel and devein shrimp, saving shells to boil for stock. Add shrimp and oysters. Bring back to boil and cook 5 minutes. Add parsley, green onions, salt and pepper to taste. Serve over hot boiled rice. (For Roux see Brown Gravy, page 38.)

*Recipe from Cookin' Cajun
Cooking School in New Orleans*

BEET SALAD WITH ONION RINGS AND GREEN ONION STICKS

2 cans sliced beets, drained	1/2 cup oil
1 medium onion, sliced	1/4 cup vinegar
6 green onions, cleaned and soaked in ice water	Pinch thyme
	Salt and Pepper to taste

Put drained beets and onion slices in a bowl. Mix oil, vinegar, thyme, salt and pepper and pour over beets and onions. Cover and refrigerate for one hour. Serve with green onion sticks as garnish.

*Recipe from Cookin' Cajun
Cooking School in New Orleans*

CREAMY POTATO SALAD

Potato salad is the traditional Cajun accompaniment to gumbo.

10 medium potatoes	1/2 cup sweet pickle relish
6 hard-boiled eggs	Salt and pepper to taste
6 green onions, chopped	1/2 cup mayonnaise
3 ribs celery, chopped fine	1 tablespoon vinegar
1 bell pepper, diced small	1 tablespoon sugar
1 small jar pimento bits	2 tablespoons French mustard
	1/2 pint cream

Peel (or not, as you prefer) and cook potatoes. Peel and dice eggs. If you want a yellow salad, remove yolks, mash, and mix with mayonnaise later. Add all chopped vegetables and sweet pickles. As you mix these together, add the proper amount of salt and pepper and check for taste. Now add yolks, vinegar, sugar, and mustard to the mayonnaise and mix thoroughly with the potatoes. Let stand in the refrigerator until cool. Now add 1/2 pint of cream. This will make a wonderfully creamy salad. Do not put salad in a deep bowl to chill as it will not cool through the center. It must be well chilled to be safe.

*Recipe from Cookin' Cajun
Cooking School in New Orleans*

Oysters with Tasso, Cream and Fettucine

Ambrosia, the Nectar of the Gods

AMBROSIA

Mix two cans of mandarin orange sections, one large can of crushed pineapple, one can of angel flake coconut, one jar of maraschino cherries without stems (drained), and enough baby marshmallows to balance the mixture. Refrigerate overnight before serving.

The old fashioned way was to leave this as is, but some people now like to add sour cream before refrigerating it. If you prefer, you can make the whole thing with fresh fruit and fresh coconut.

FRIED OYSTER CANAPÉS WITH FISH VELOUTÉ SAUCE

Dip fresh oysters in batter and fry in deep fat until crisp. Place on toast rounds and serve with a Fish Velouté (velvety) Sauce.

Fish Velouté Sauce: Melt 3 tablespoons butter and gradually smooth in 3 tablespoons flour. Slowly add 1 cup hot fish broth (strained) and continue to stir. After sauce thickens, bring to a boil and then quickly lower the heat. Simmer a few minutes more, add 1/3 cup heavy cream and salt to taste and finish heating.

Hors d'Oeuvres on the Paddle Wheelers

The Natchez Boat is one of the older paddle-wheelers, and an institution on the Mississippi at New Orleans. Most of the River Boats serve buffet lunches or dinners, or snacks for in between times. There is dancing on the boats and the hors d'oeuvres and desserts are always interesting. Here we have also pulled some of the hors d'oeuvres recipes from other pages in our Cajun cookbook.

FROMAGE DE TÊTE
(Head Cheese)

1 pound heavy veal	1 1/2 teaspoons paprika
1 pound pork	1 teaspoon sage
4 pig's feet (not pickled)	1 teaspoon basil
4 calves feet (not pickled)	1 teaspoon powdered bay leaf
4 onions	4 sprigs parsley
2 stalks celery	Salt and cayenne pepper
6 green onions	to taste

(Head cheese is really just another form of a French Paté.)

Boil all meats in a gallon of salted water to which a tablespoon of lemon juice and vinegar have been added. Cook for 3 to 4 hours until meat is falling from bones. Remove meat and chop, grind, or shred, as you prefer. Strain broth and add to meat. Add vegetables, which have all been finely chopped, and seasonings. Vegetables can be sautéed in a little butter before adding to the broth. Continue cooking everything for 20 minutes. Pour into loaf pan or individual molds. Chill and set thoroughly. Turn out and garnish with parsley. Slice thin and serve with crackers.

Head cheese is usually made pretty hot, and country people, when they are butchering, use meat from the head, feet, tongue, and heart of the pig. It can be purchased in the stores in Louisiana.

SAUSAGE CANAPÉS WITH MUSTARD DRESSING

There are two types of sausage that are very popular in South Louisiana. Boudin (Boo-dan) is made of pork liver and rice, and Andouille (Ahn-doo-ee) is a very firm, spicy, dark red sausage. Cut slices of both, at least 1/4 inch thick, and fry until brown. Drain off fat and place on toast rounds. Top with a mustard dressing.

Mustard Dressing: Put 1 tablespoon butter, 1/2 teaspoon salt, 6 tablespoons dry mustard, 1/2 cup heavy cream and a beaten egg into the top of a double boiler. Heat over boiling water until thick, stirring constantly.

(Author's Recipes)

MARINATED THREE BEAN SALAD

1 can French cut green beans	1/2 cup salad oil
1 can cut wax beans	1/2 cup vinegar
1 can kidney beans	2 tablespoons sugar
1 red onion	1 teaspoon celery seed
1/2 bell pepper	2 tablespoons chopped parsley
1 small jar pimento	Salt and pepper to taste

Drain all beans. Cut onion in half and slice as thinly as possible in half rings. Cut pepper in half and slice in half rings. Mix beans, onions, pepper and pimento together. In a separate bowl, mix all of the ingredients for the dressing. Pour over bean mixture and refrigerate overnight before serving.

(from Rose Marie Greely)

Fromage de tête

Paddle Your Own Canoe ... to the Buffet.

The chefs on the Natchez have put together some of their buffet style food and displayed it in a little green rowboat. At the prow of the boat is a luscious bowl of Ambrosia, an old New Orleans favorite. Sliced Roast Beef is displayed with wedges of Ripe Tomatoes; next, a bowl of Corn Vinaigrette and another of Sweet and Sour Beet Salad; a tray of Ham Roll-ups are banded with strips of pimento; a tray of Sliced Turkey is surrounded by Buttered Corn, and lastly comes a Three Bean Salad garnished with Tomato Wedges.

SWEET AND SOUR BEET SALAD

1 can sliced beets	1/4 cup vinegar
1 large onion	Salt and pepper to taste
1/2 cup olive oil	1/4 cup sweet pickle
1/4 cup brown sugar	relish (optional)

Cut beet slices in half if you want more manageable pieces. Slice onion into thin rings. Mix all other ingredients with oil and pour over beets and onions. Marinate overnight for full flavor.

HAM ROLL-UPS

Spread slices of ham with Philadelphia cream cheese. Lay a stalk of asparagus at one end of the cheese, and roll the ham around it. Wrap with a strip of pimento or red bell pepper.

CORN VINAIGRETTE

2 cans corn niblets	1/2 cup light oil
1 red bell pepper or	1 tablespoon sugar
pimento, diced	1/2 cup white Worcestershire
1 small onion, chopped	Sauce
1 small cucumber, sliced	Salt and cayenne pepper

Mix corn niblets, red bell pepper bits, and finely chopped onion. Mix other ingredients, pour over corn, and thoroughly mix together with other vegetables. Place in shallow bowl and place a row of thin cucumber slices around the edge. Garnish center with strips of red pepper.

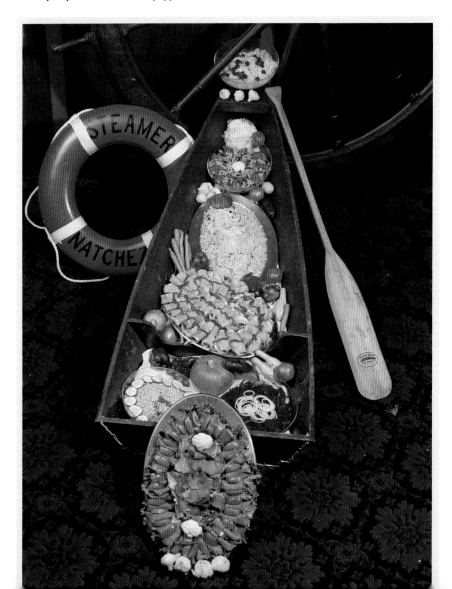

One Last Bowl of Gumbo ... and then Home!

We told you earlier that there were a myriad of recipes for Gumbo. Well, here is one more—Chicken and Andouille Filé Gumbo. Andouille is a very firmly packed red sausage, that is well seasoned and gives an excellent flavor to whatever it is cooked with, whether gumbo, jambalaya or vegetables. In this recipe, it particularly perks up the flavor of the chicken, and blends nicely with all of the seasonings. Pierre found another dish in New Orleans he jus' love, that "Bananas Foster" they pour over that Creme Glacée (Ice Cream), so his Maman took that recipe home, too.

BANANAS FOSTER

3 bananas	1 teaspoon vanilla
1 stick butter	1/2 cup rum
1 cup brown sugar	1/2 cup banana liqueur

Slice the bananas in three slices lengthwise, then cut in halves. Melt the butter in a skillet or frying pan, add brown sugar (you may also add 1/2 teaspoon cinnamon if desired) and cook over low heat, stirring into a thick paste. Add vanilla and banana liqueur and stir well with the sugar and butter mixture. Cook about 5 minutes. (Mixture will bubble while cooking.)

Heat the rum in a metal cup or ladle, ignite, and pour over bananas. (Rum will have a faint blue flame in the cup and will flame up when poured over the bananas.) Stir well to blend, then serve mixture with pieces of bananas over vanilla ice cream. (Ice cream will do better if scooped into balls and frozen ahead of time and bowls are chilled so both are very cold when Bananas Foster is ready to serve.

All Recipes on this page are from the Cookin' Cajun Cooking School in New Orleans

Chicken and Andouille Filé Gumbo

CHICKEN AND ANDOUILLE FILÉ GUMBO

1 fryer, cut up	3 cloves garlic, minced
1 1/2 lbs. Andouille	Salt and pepper
1/2 cup oil	Cayenne pepper
1/2 cup flour	Thyme
2 cups chopped onion	Bay leaves
1/2 cup chopped bell pepper	Filé powder
1 cup chopped celery	Green onions
6 cups chicken stock	Parsley

In a heavy Dutch oven, brown chicken and set aside. In same pot, make a dark brown roux with remaining oil and flour. Add onions and brown. Add bell pepper and celery. Cook 5 more minutes. Add stock, garlic, and seasonings (to taste) except for filé powder. Bring to a boil, then turn to simmer. Add chicken and sausage and simmer for 2 or 3 hours. Serve over boiled rice. Garnish with green onion and parsley. Add filé powder at the table.

FRIED EGGPLANT FINGERS

1 eggplant, cut in finger-long strips	Tabasco (to taste)
1/2 cup flour (seasoned with salt, pepper and cayenne)	Seasoned bread crumbs (Chef seasons with salt, pepper and cayenne)
2 eggs	Salt to taste
1/2 cup milk	Pepper to taste
	Oil (for frying)

Salt eggplant fingers and let sit in colander 20 minutes. Rinse and dry well. Dip the fingers into flour, then dip into a mixture of the eggs, milk and Tabasco. Dip into bread crumbs. Deepfry slowly on both sides.

There Goes the Showboat.

It is time for everyone to head for home, and the paddle wheel of the Creole Queen is ready to start churning up the Mississippi, but not before one last grand meal. The other dishes are a perfect compliment to the Chicken and Andouille Filé Gumbo. Fried Eggplant Fingers, Mardi Gras Salad and a cooling Praline Parfait should satisfy any tired Cajun. The menu was again put together by the Cookin' Cajun Cooking School.

MARDI GRAS SALAD

Wash one head of lettuce well, dry, and tear into pieces. Slice one yellow bell pepper into long narrow strips. Wash 1/8 of a head of purple cabbage, drain well and slice into long thin pieces.

Mix a Creole Mustard Salad Dressing by blending 2 tablespoons Creole Mustard (a dark mustard), 2 tablespoons red wine or sherry vinegar, one small onion, peeled and quartered, add salt and pepper to taste in a blender. Slowly pour in oil while blending. Arrange salad with lettuce in the bottom of the bowl and purple cabbage and yellow bell pepper strips scattered over the top. Pour 3/4 cup dressing over the salad.

PRALINE PARFAIT

Praline Topping: Caramelize 1 cup brown sugar, add 1 cup chopped pecans that have been toasted, a few grains of salt, and 1 cup dark corn syrup. Let mixture simmer a few minutes, turn off heat, and let cool. Layer ice cream in parfait glasses, then praline topping, and repeat until glasses are filled to the top. Garnish with a maraschino cherry and whipping cream if desired. If you do not wish to make the topping, you can order it.

All Recipes on this page are from the Cookin' Cajun Cooking School in New Orleans

(The following Cajun and Creole gourmet items can be ordered from Creole Delicacies at the Cookin' Cajun Cooking School in New Orleans.)

Creole Mustard
Praline Topping (See recipe above)
Gumbo Filé Powder
Hot Pepper Jelly
Creole Delicacies Pralines: Original, Chocolate, Rum or Chewie
Pecanfections: Sugared pecan halves in Orange, Cinnamon, Rum or Praline Flavors.

(See inside front cover for address)

51

Back Down to the Bayou Country ...

Everything is great—down on the bayou. Nice to be back, although New Orleans was fun. When the nets are out, turtles can be caught, and although it may sound "fishy" to the visitor, turtle meat is very tasty, and is best in a rich soup or a dark sauce piquante. Oudrey's Restaurant at Belle River fixed some fine food for us. The Turtle Sauce Piquante is rich, the fried Crab Fingers are crisp, and the Chef Salad with slivered Cheese and Ham, and Wedges of Tomatoes and Eggs is fresh and wonderful. Nicely browned large French Fries, a plate of crunchy Fried Crawfish, and an Oyster Cocktail make the day complete.

FRIED CRAWFISH

Beat two eggs into a cup of milk. Add salt and pepper and stir in well. Dip the crawfish into the battering mixture and then into a bowl of finely ground cornmeal ("fish fry"). Drop into hot deep fat and fry until crispy brown. When tiny crawfish are fried like this, they are called "Cajun Popcorn" and are eaten with the fingers.

CAJUN FRENCH FRIED "PATATES"

For true tasty fried potatoes done in the Cajun manner, dust the raw potato sticks with salt and cayenne pepper. Then drop in hot deep fat and fry until golden brown. The "fried in" seasoning makes them wonderful and spicy.

OYSTER COCKTAIL

1 cup ketchup	1 tablespoon lemon juice
2 tablespoons horseradish sauce	Dash of Tabasco sauce (or more if desired)
1 tablespoon Pickapeppa	1 tablespoon Worcestershire sauce
Salt and garlic powder to taste	1 tablespoon tarragon vinegar

Mix all ingredients together until they are perfectly blended. Taste and see if it suits you. You can add a dash of sugar if you wish. If you have homemade ketchup it will be even better. Freshly ground horseradish is great, but it is really hot, so be careful. If you have fresh tarragon in your garden, by all means make your own tarragon vinegar. It will taste 3 times as good as "store bought". Make ahead and chill at least a day. Better yet, make a larger quantity and keep it on hand. It will keep for several weeks because of all the seasonings, if it is in an airtight container. Use on oysters, shrimp, crabs, crawfish, or flaked fish.

(Author's Recipes)

Fried Crawfish and Fried "Patates".

FRIED CRAB FINGERS

Make crab "fingers" out of the cooked crab claws by breaking off the stationary portion of the claw. Leave the meat attached but handle it carefully so that it does not break off. Dip in milk and drain. Season with salt and red or black pepper. Dip in finely ground cornmeal "breading" and fry in deep fat until nicely browned. I do not like heavy breading on these delicate morsels. To eat, pick them up in your fingers while nice and hot and just pull the meat off the central cartilage with your teeth. Delicious!

TURTLE SAUCE PIQUANTE

2 pounds fresh turtle meat, cut into large bite size pieces and sautéed in butter until nicely browned. This recipe may also be used for chicken, shrimp, crawfish, venison, or almost any other meat.

4 tablespoons oil	1 teaspoon minced garlic
4 tablespoons flour	1 tablespoon lemon zest
4 medium onions, chopped	2 quarts water
1/2 cup chopped celery	2 cans tomatoes
1/2 cup chopped bell pepper	1 small can tomato paste
1/2 cup chopped green onions	1/4 cup dark steak sauce
1/3 cup chopped parsley	1 tablespoon sugar
1/2 cup mushroom pieces with their liquor	Salt and cayenne pepper
	Tabasco to taste

Make a roux with the oil and flour. Put the flour in the hot oil and stir it constantly until it darkens to a rich brown. Before adding any water, add the tomato paste and let it darken with the roux. Add all of the vegetables and the lemon zest to the roux and stir in well. Turn the heat down, simmer a minute or two, then add the water gradually, smoothing it in as it cooks. Add the tomatoes, steak sauce, sugar and seasoning and continue to cook. Add the turtle meat and simmer until turtle meat is tender and roux is well cooked. Correct for seasoning. Serve with hot fluffy rice.

La Pirogue ... She Float on the Dew!

The Pirogue has been one of the greatest treasures of people who dwell near swamps and marshes. Originally they were carved and hollowed out from a single log, but now they are built as a regular boat is, but they are light, and narrow and draw little water. The Cajuns have an expression that they need so little water to travel on that they can float on the dew. It gives a man great comfort just to have one tied up in his front yard, among the water hyacinth leaves. We found this scene down near Pierre Part.

FESTIVE RICE SALAD

3 cups cooked rice	1/4 cup chopped bell pepper
1 cup creamy cucumber	1/4 cup chopped pimento
dressing	1/4 cup chopped boiled eggs
1/2 cup chopped green	1/3 cup sweet pickle relish
onions with small tops	1/4 cup chopped parsley
1/3 cup finely chopped celery	Salt and black or cayenne
	pepper to taste

Mixing all ingredients with the rice while it is still hot makes the flavor of the vegetables blend even better than waiting for it to cool. Pack into a bowl and chill. Invert the bowl and center salad on plate before removing the bowl. Decorate with strips of pepper and pimento. A nice touch is to surround it with chopped pieces of cucumber in the same dressing. Dust lightly with paprika.

SPICED PEACHES

Drain syrup from a can of whole peaches and save. Add half again as much wine vinegar to the syrup. Insert two cloves into each whole peach. Add one stick cinnamon, 1 teaspoon pepper-corns, mace and allspice to taste. Bring syrup to boil and add the fruit. Remove from heat, cover and cool. Let fruit stand in syrup and refrigerate overnight. It is a good idea to shake the peaches or turn them gently a few times.

(Author's Recipes)

BLACK-EYED PEAS WITH MUSHROOMS

1 pound black-eyed peas	1 teaspoon basil
3 quarts water	1 hambone, if possible
1 cup chopped green onions	1 pound 1/2-inch slices
1 chopped bell pepper	of smoked sausage
2 ribs celery, chopped	Salt and black or red pepper
2 bay leaves	1/4 cup chopped parsley

Place bone, water, peas, and all ingredients except the parsley, in a heavy pot and cook for an hour. Meanwhile, brown the sausage slices well and drain. Add them to the beans and continue cooking until creamy. Addition of a little oil helps the creaminess if lean ham or pork are used instead of sausage. If more water is needed during the cooking, add cold water. Any kind of pork may be substituted for the sausage, including ham, salt meat, pickled pork, or even andouille sausage (pronounced ahn-doo'-ee). Black-eyed peas are usually served over hot rice. However, a soup may be made of black-eyed peas, or red or white beans by just adding more water.

What Can't You Put Crawfish In?

*Answer: Almost **nothing.** Crawfish are smaller than most shrimp, but they are so tasty that they are enjoyed in combination with almost every kind of food except desserts. They are great in salads, stews, gumbos, pies, jambalaya, and ad infinitum. Chef Diane Ourso at The Cabin Restaurant at Burnside, near the Mississippi, has even put them in a huge yellow omelette, and they are delicious. You will notice that we do not call them Crayfish in Louisiana. Sometimes they are called mudbugs, or crawdaddies, but usually we just call them **Crawfish.** Sometimes we only boil them, and that satisfies our taste very well.*

Crawfish Omelette

CRAWFISH OMELETTE

First, make a sauce with chopped up stewed tomatoes, tomato paste, and chopped onion, bell pepper and parsley. Put a handful of peeled crawfish in this and cook until pink.

Now, beat four eggs lightly till blended, and mix in 4 table-spoons of milk or cream and seasoning of salt, pepper, and any herb you might like. Melt 2 tablespoons of butter in a hot omelet pan. When melted, pour in the egg mixture gently and reduce heat. As the omelet cooks, the proper procedure is to lift the edges with a spatula, letting some of the raw egg mixture run underneath until all of it is creamy and starting to set. When almost ready, pour the crawfish with its sauce over half of it. Now fold the other half over and serve immediately while still hot. This is a very tasty dish for breakfast, lunch, or supper.

PAIN PERDU
(Lost Bread)

No book on Cajun Cooking that considers breakfast would be complete without "Lost Bread". (French toast to the rest of the world.)

8 slices stale sliced bread or French bread	1/2 cup sugar
	1 cup cooking oil
1 small can evaporated milk	1/2 teaspoon vanilla
6 beaten eggs	Cane syrup (from sugar cane)

Beat sugar into eggs, and then milk and vanilla. Coat both sides of each slice of bread, drain and drop immediately into hot oil. Brown nicely on both sides. These may be served with powdered sugar or syrup, honey, or molasses, but most Cajuns prefer cane syrup. This is a fine dish for supper as well as for breakfast.

Good Ole' Country Cajun Cookin'

When served for lunch, the Crawfish Omelette goes well with Yellow Cornbread; a Colossal Salad with King Crab Meat and Shrimp, Cucumber, Lettuce, Tomatoes and Peppers; a small dish of Red Beans with Ham, Dirty Rice, Curly Q Fries, and Yellow Bread Pudding. We set it all up by the little lagoon in front of The Cabin, right by the huge alligator that has been carved out of a 32 foot log with a chain saw.

COUNTRY BREAD PUDDING

2 cups torn up stale French bread	1/4 cup melted butter
	1/2 teaspoon vanilla
2 cups scalded milk	1 cup raisins
4 eggs, slightly beaten	1 cup chopped apple
1/2 cup sugar	1/4 teaspoon salt

Soak the bread pieces in the scalded milk and let cool.

Add all of the other ingredients and mix in with the soaked bread. Bake in a greased baking dish at 325° until brown and crusty. (Yellow food coloring may be added.)

MOLASSES CORNBREAD

3/4 cup cornmeal	1/4 cup molasses
1 cup flour	1 cup milk
2 teaspoons baking powder	1 egg, well beaten
3/4 teaspoon salt	2 tablespoons cooking oil

Mix and sift the cornmeal, flour, baking powder and salt together. Add molasses, milk, and egg. Heat the cooking oil in the baking pan which you intend to use. When hot (and don't let it catch fire), pour it into the cornmeal mix. It will spew and bubble. Then pour the cornbread into the hot greased pan. This will make the crust nice. Bake in a hot oven, 425°, for about 20 minutes.

COLOSSAL SEAFOOD SALAD

In our picture, this tremendous salad is arranged in a huge bowl in the shape of a clam shell. Twin piles of shredded King Crab-meat and cold shrimp are surrounded by cucumber slices, fancy cut tomatoes, pepper rings, and lemon slices, all on a crisp and curly bed of lettuce.

BUTTER PECAN CHEESECAKE
(Napped with a Caramel Sauce)

Toast one cup of finely chopped pecans in 1/4 cup butter until lightly browned. Add 1/2 cup sugar and heat with pecans until caramelized. Add a very small amount of cream and stir it in so that the caramel will not harden, and heat. Allow to cool.

Mix together 1/2 stick of butter (at room temperature), 1/4 cup sugar and 1 1/2 cups graham cracker crumbs. Press mixture on the bottom and a fourth of the way up the sides of a spring form pan.

Filling:

1 1/2 pounds Philadelphia Cream Cheese (at room temperature)	1 cup sugar
	4 eggs
	2 teaspoons almond flavoring

Beat cream cheese well, add sugar and beat thoroughly. Add eggs, one at a time, beating extremely well after each. Add almond flavoring. Gently fold in the butter pecan mixture, and carefully pour the entire amount into the graham cracker crust. Bake at 375° for 25 to 30 minutes, cool for 5 minutes and spread on a topping made of 1 1/2 cups sour cream mixed with 2 tablespoons sugar and 1 tablespoon vanilla flavoring. Bake at 400° for 5 minutes. Refrigerate overnight. Serve by pouring a thin layer of caramel sauce into a shallow dessert plate and placing a piece of the cheesecake in the center of the sauce.

To make the caramel sauce, put a cup of sugar in a heavy-bottomed pan and swirl it over very low heat. Do not stir. It will melt slowly and make a clear golden syrup that will set off the cheese-cake beautifully.

(Author's Recipes)

55

Andouille Islands for Breakfast

Here is our famous Andouille (pronounced ahn-doo-ee) again, used in still a different way. The Cabin serves this enormous breakfast plate with three huge slices of Andouille Sausage alternated with three Fried Eggs; served up with a Hashed Brown Potato Patty; Parslied Grits, Cantaloupe Slices, Sausage Links with an Orange Basket, and Buttermilk Biscuits with Preserved Figs. The Coffee, of course, is either a demitasse of the strong black kind or a mug of "café au lait" with hot milk. You may have your choice of a spicy Tabasco Bloody Mary or a cool Screwdriver in tall glass steins. The backdrop for this scene is the Burnside General Store, which is attached to The Cabin. Then how about a ride in the skiff?

Andouille Islands for Breakfast

ANDOUILLE ISLANDS

Fry thick slices of Andouille sausage on both sides until well browned. Fry eggs in a separate skillet. Place three eggs on a plate, sunnyside up and place three slices of Andouille between the eggs. Garnish with a slice of orange and parsley. A "healthy" man-size breakfast.

HASHED BROWN POTATOES

Heat 5 tablespoons bacon fat or oil in a heavy skillet. Dice 4 cooked potatoes into 1/4 inch pieces. Use 1/4 cup diced onions. Put the potatoes in when the pan is hot and spread across the bottom. Lower heat immediately and add the onions on the top. Salt and pepper the mixture. Cook until the bottom side is well browned but do not burn. Press down as the potatoes cook with spatula. Cut into quarters and turn each quarter over to brown the other side. Press down again. Serve immediately.

BUTTERMILK BISCUITS

2 cups sifted flour	1/2 cup cream of tartar
2 teaspoons baking powder	2 teaspoons sugar
1/2 teaspoon salt	1/2 cup shortening
1/2 teaspoon soda	2/3 cup buttermilk

Preheat oven to 450°. Sift dry ingredients. Cut in shortening with a pastry cutter or two knives. Pat and roll to desired thickness. Cut large or small biscuits and bake on an ungreased cookie sheet for 10 to 12 minutes.

CRACKLIN' CORNBREAD

"Cracklin's" (cracklings) are made from cut up pieces of pork fat with skin, which are fried in deep fat until brown and crispy like potato chips. For this recipe they should be cut small. Crisp fried bacon bits, well drained, may be substituted.

3/4 cup yellow cornmeal	3/4 teaspoon salt
1 cup flour	1 cup buttermilk
1/3 cup sugar	1 well beaten egg
1 teaspoon soda	2 tablespoons cooking oil
2 teaspoons cream of tartar	1/2 cup cracklings

Mix the dried ingredients, add the buttermilk and egg, and then the cracklings or bacon. Pour the oil into the pan in which the cornbread is to be baked. Heat in the 425° oven which is being preheated, until the oil is very hot, but don't let it catch fire. Immediately pour it into the batter, stir quickly, and pour the batter back into the hot pan. It will crackle, and will make a better crust. Bake for 20 minutes. This entire procedure can be done in an iron skillet instead of a baking pan.

SWEET AND SOUR RED CABBAGE

Pick the smallest head of red cabbage you can find, because this always makes much more than you think it will. Shred finely in the food processor. Slice one red onion finely in long slivers, and cut up two peeled apples into thin slices. Place the red onions and the apples in the bottom of the pan, then add the cabbage over them. Cook, uncovered, until tender, stirring gently now and then. Add vinegar (a flavored vinegar or raspberry vinegar is nice), and brown sugar carefully, a tablespoon at a time and taste as you proceed to balance the sweet and sour flavor to your own taste. Add 2 tablespoons butter or margarine, salt and lemon pepper as you like it, and a little nutmeg and cayenne if you wish. This makes a colorful and very tasty dish.

(Author's Recipes)

Pan Fried Red Snapper, Fried Shrimp and Country Fried Steak ...

We displayed some fine Cajun Country fare on a bateau in the courtyard of The Cabin, and allowed a little alligator to sun himself there. The Pan Fried Red Snapper is pretty much like a fish you would fry in a big, white hot, black iron skillet over a campfire when you go fishing. The Fried Shrimp have been dipped in a thick fluffy batter that is typical of the Cabin's cooking, and the Country Fried Steak is about as country as you can get, and is served with cole slaw and a tomato rose.

COUNTRY FRIED STEAK

Cut round steaks into smaller steaks, pound till they are thin, but do not break the fibers. Season well with salt and pepper on both sides, pat seasoning into meat with hand, and dip in batter made by beating 2 eggs and thinning with a little milk. Then dip in flour or bread crumbs and fry in about 3 inches of vegetable oil until crispy brown. If you are using bread crumbs, Parmesan cheese may be added to the mixture.

CREAM GRAVY

3 tablespoons butter
3 tablespoons flour
1/2 cup beef bouillon
1 cup heavy cream
1 egg, beaten
Salt to taste
Freshly ground pepper
to taste

Heat butter on low heat and add flour. Add bouillon slowly to butter/flour mixture, smoothing it in and allowing it to thicken some. Beat egg into cream, and slowly add the cream and egg mixture to the gravy. Add seasoning and continue to cook until gravy is the thickness you desire. Keep heat low and do not allow gravy to scorch or darken.

It's Just Your Basic Cajun Country

It seems that after seeing the little Acadian cottages in South Louisiana, everyone wants to go home and have one of his own. Many people do acquire the plans to build an authentic copy for a camp. Something takes us back to the simple life. Simple food, too, is best. Most of our recipes are done in the very basic style of Cajun Cooking. Some of today's so-called "Cajun Cooking" in non-Cajun restaurants has evolved into overly rich, layered concoctions with combinations of different foods and lots of heavy sauces, to the point of becoming oppressive.

BATTER FRIED SHRIMP

1 pound fresh shrimp, peeled and deveined	1/2 cup buttermilk
	Salt
1 cup flour	Cayenne pepper
1 whole egg, beaten	Peanut oil

Be sure the cleaned shrimp are dry, and season them well. Make up the batter as you prefer, thick or thin. (To vary, add more or less flour to the recipe. Or, dip the shrimp in the buttermilk batter, and then dip again in a bowl of plain flour and shake off the excess, if you like a heavier batter. Heat oil to 365° and fry the shrimp in deep fat.

OLD-FASHIONED HUSH PUPPIES

1 cup yellow cornmeal	1/4 cup milk
2 teaspoons baking powder	Cayenne pepper to taste
1/2 teaspoon salt	1 medium onion, chopped
1 egg	

Mix together the dry ingredients, including the onion. Break in the egg and beat "good-heartedly". Add milk and form into round flattened patties. In order to give a larger crunchy surface and to prevent the center from becoming too heavy, punch a "finger-hole" in the center. Then drop into hot deep fat, preferably the smoking pot that fish has just been fried in. Serve hot. (You can also drop these by the spoonful.)

CONTEMPORARY HUSH PUPPIES

Use the above recipe but add 1/2 cup flour and 2 teaspoons sugar. Substitute 1/2 cup buttermilk for the 1/4 cup milk, and omit the red pepper. This will make a softer, lighter batter. Drop by heaping teaspoonfuls into hot oil and fry until golden brown.

PAN FRIED RED SNAPPER

8 Red Snapper fillets	Seasoning salt
1 stick butter	Crushed rosemary
1 stick oleo	Crushed tarragon
Black peppercorns	Hungarian rose paprika

Be sure the fillets are not too thick. Melt the butter and the oleo together and brush both sides of the fillet thickly with the mixture. This will keep your fillets from drying out when you fry them. Coat with freshly ground black pepper (or use cayenne or lemon pepper if you prefer). You can make up your own mixture of seasoning salt with any vegetable salts or ground herbs that you like, or buy your favorite kind. Crumble the crushed rosemary and tarragon over the fillets and dust with paprika. Pat in and let stand.

This procedure makes a lot of smoke in the kitchen, so build a large and very hot fire of charcoal outdoors and when it is really hot, place a large iron frying pan close to the coals. Do not put the fish in until the pan is smoking hot. Lift the fillets into it quickly, fry in minutes, and turn quickly. It will fry a very dark brown, look gorgeous, and taste even better, with a great smoky flavor. You may think it is going to burn, but it won't if you watch it carefully. Be ready to serve it immediately.

STRAWBERRY SHORTCAKE

See recipe for Peach Shortcake on page 17. Cut strawberries in halves, saving a few for a garnish, sugar, and let stand awhile to draw out the juice. Serve as described in recipe

(Author's Recipes)

Let's Have a Shellfish Boil!

The most basic common denominator used as a reason for Cajun people to get together is a shellfish boil. It does not matter whether it is Crawfish, Shrimp or Crabs. One buys a package of Crab Boil seasoning that is full of bay leaves, peppercorns, cayenne pepper, and everything imaginable; heat up a big pot of water; dump it in with whatever you plan to eat in the way of shellfish; and add some corn on the cob, whole onions, baby new potatoes, and some lemon halves to the pot; and everyone will follow their Cajun noses to the pot. It would be a good idea to have some chips, some French bread and some watermelon on hand. Tomatoes stuffed with Egg Salad are just pleasant extras. French Bread can be purchased in the shapes of alligators and crawfish.

TOMATOES STUFFED WITH EGG SALAD

Peel hard-boiled eggs, and separate the yolks from the whites. Chop whites. Mash yolks with a fork and gradually mix in a little prepared mustard (yellow or dark) and a little mayonnaise until it is creamy. Add salt and pepper, chopped egg whites, drained sweet pickle relish, and a small amount of finely chopped onion or celery if you like.

I am leaving the amounts up to your individual taste. Cut out tops of small tomatoes, carefully scoop out insides, and stuff with egg salad. Arrange on a platter of lettuce.

ASPARAGUS HOLLANDAISE

Wash asparagus and beginning at the bottom, bend gently, working your fingers up until it snaps at the tender part. Throw the bottoms away. Plunge into a large amount of boiling water and begin to test the bottom ends with a fork after 5 minutes. You may need to cook a little longer, depending on the size of the spears. Drain well and serve with the Hollandaise Sauce.

Hollandaise Sauce: Beat together 4 egg yolks and one tablespoon each of lemon juice and tarragon vinegar in a double boiler over heating (but not boiling) water. Heat until thickened. Remove from heat and whisk in one-half pound of melted butter, pouring in a thin stream. (You may need to add a tablespoon or two of hot water if the consistency is too thick.) Season with salt, white pepper, and paprika and hold in wide mouth thermos until serving time.

SHELLFISH BOIL
WITH CORN ON THE COB, WHOLE ONIONS AND BABY NEW POTATOES

The most important things needed for a shellfish boil are a very large pot (at least 10 gallons) over an outdoor fire, and a supply of commercial "Crab Boil", not always easily obtained outside of Louisiana. It is a mixture of peppercorns, bay leaves, and other herbs. Use it according to directions on the box. If you do not have it, use 1/2 box of salt for 6 gallons of water, and about 4 ounces of Cayenne (red) pepper. Cut several lemons in halves and throw in the pot, for the proper flavor for seafood. For a picnic or party, you will want to add corn on the cob (usually cut in halves), baby new potatoes, and small whole onions. They pick up the flavor of the Crab Boil seasoning and are hot, spicy, and wonderful. You can cook large quantities, or different shellfish in separate batches. Cook crawfish until they are bright red (about 15 minutes or more), crabs about 10 minutes, and shrimp until they are pink (about 5 minutes or a little more), but not too long. Spread newspapers or brown paper on picnic tables, and serve while everything is hot, as it comes out of the pot. Then let everyone peel their favorite shellfish, and make a mess to their hearts content. Afterward, just roll up the papers and put them in a plastic bag.

AVOCADO PIROGUE

Fill half of a large, ripe avocado with lump crabmeat which has been tossed in a dressing made by adding lemon juice and a tiny amount of tomato ketchup to mayonnaise. Salt and pepper lightly. Wipe the surface of the avocado with a little lemon so it won't turn brown. Serve on a bed of lettuce.

(Author's Recipes)

There Comes That Alligator Again!

Chef Eric Van Camp at The Pilot House Restaurant prepared a rare delicacy for us, Alligator Sauce Piquante. Don't grimace. It is really good, just as good as eating chicken. He also prepared a Red Fish Fillet with a Courtbouillon Sauce, and an Avocado Pirogue filled with Crabmeat, and garnished with Tomatoes, Eggs, and Pickled Okra. The Asparagus is sauced with Hollandaise and the Butter Pecan Cheesecake is napped with a Caramel Sauce. Tiny Fried Crawfish are often called Cajun Popcorn and eaten that way, and we served them in a compote surrounded by lemon slices.

TINY FRIED CRAWFISH
(Often called Cajun Popcorn)

I would suggest frying the little bite size crawfish in the Japanese manner. The cajun way would be to use flour on these, but try using cornstarch instead for a very light batter. Beat an egg with a little water. Season the crawfish, dip in the egg and then in the cornstarch, and fry quickly. Pile up in the center of a pretty compote and arrange a row of thin slices of lemon around the edge. Serve hot.

You might try to find a new item at the market—soft shelled crawfish, and fry them in the same way. These are like soft shelled crabs, and are caught when the shell is changing and is, therefore, soft. They are delicious, but because they have to be sorted out from the others at a specific time, they are hard to find and very expensive.

ALLIGATOR SAUCE PIQUANTE

See recipe for Turtle Sauce Piquante on page 52. Buy very sweet fresh alligator meat and cut into bite size pieces. Sauté until nicely browned, and proceed as with turtle recipe.

BROILED RED FISH FILLET

Salt and pepper fillets. Sprinkle lightly with fresh or dry thyme, and pat seasoning in. Dust with a small amount of flour, not a heavy coating, and gently pat flour and seasonings into fish. Heat a small amount of butter or oleo in a sauté pan but do not let it brown. Broil fish very quickly on one side and then the other. Serve immediately.

Serve this with a Courtbouillon Sauce if you like. See page 16 for recipe.

TARTAR SAUCE

1 cup mayonnaise	1 tablespoon sweet or dill
1 tablespoon small capers	pickle
2 green onions, minced	1 tablespoon minced parsley
	1 tablespoon lemon juice

Blend ingredients in a bowl. Add salt and pepper as desired.
(Author's Recipes)

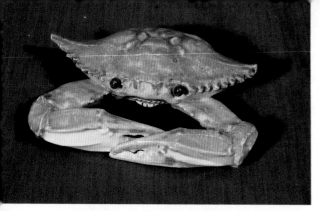

Help the Shrimp Fleet ...

Eric fixed some Shrimp Stuffed with a Crabmeat Dressing, which is about as tasty a treat as one can find, and we also fixed Shrimp Cocktails in little pottery shrimp dishes. (You will notice that we Southerners do not add an "s" to the plural of Shrimp. To say Shrimps seems a little gauche to our Southern ears and we may turn our noses up, but not really. We're a friendly folk!)

Stuffed Shrimp and Shrimp Cocktails ...

SHRIMP STUFFED WITH CRABMEAT

Peel and devein the largest fresh shrimp you can find but leave the tails on. Open down the back into a modified butterfly but do not flatten, and do not separate the halves. Stuff with crabmeat mixture. (See stuffed crab recipe on page 22.) Press sides together tightly around the stuffing. Chill or freeze so that they will retain their shape. Dip in flour, then in a batter made by beating an egg and a cup of milk together, and then dredge well in the flour one more time. Fry in deep fat at 375° till golden.

CRABMEAT AU GRATIN

5 tablespoons butter	1 1/2 cups grated cheddar
4 tablespoons flour	cheese
1 cup half and half	2 tablespoons dry white wine
2 eggs, well beaten	1 tablespoon Worcestershire
1 to 2 pounds lump	Sauce
crabmeat	Dash of Tabasco
	Salt to taste

Melt butter, gently stir in flour, add milk slowly and smooth in gently. Beat some of the hot mixture into the eggs gradually and when smooth, add back into the sauce. (Add a little milk if sauce is too thick.) Remove from heat and add crabmeat, cheddar cheese, wine and seasonings. Put the whole creamy mixture into a 1 1/2 quart casserole or into six individual ramekins. Bread crumb topping is optional. Bake at 350° till bubbly.

STUFFED FLOUNDER WITH CRABMEAT DRESSING

Use one whole flounder per person. Make a pocket for stuffing by cutting through the skin in the middle of the fish, beginning at the fins and following the bone down the center. Make up a seasoning mix, of salt, cayenne and black pepper, tarragon, and onion salt, and rub into the cavity and all over the skin of the fish on both sides. Stuff with crabmeat stuffing. (See recipe for stuffed crabs on page 22.) Top with bread crumbs. Put the flounder in an oiled baking pan that has been preheated under the broiler. Put the pan back under the hot broiler and leave for 20 minutes until cooked through and nicely browned. Serve plain or with Hollandaise Sauce.

FRIED SOFT SHELLED CRABS

1 or 2 crabs per person	Seasoned flour
1 cup milk	Oil for deep frying
1/2 cup water	Cayenne pepper to taste
2 eggs, beaten	Salt to taste

To clean soft shelled crabs, lift up pointed end of shell and remove the spongy debris in there. With a sharp knife, cut out eyes and mouth of crab. Turn over and remove the apron from the underside of the crab. Wash in cold water.

In a bowl, mix milk, water, eggs, and salt and pepper to taste. Dip each crab in the milk, then dredge in seasoned flour. Deep fry until golden brown. Garnish with lumps of herbed crabmeat, cucumber slices and half a lemon. Serve immediately.